Risotto Crime

Christamaria Fiedler

Risotto Crime

Aus dem Deutschen
von Sally-Ann Spencer

Thienemann

– 1 –

There was no doubt about it: they were going to be late.

Isy **glanced** impatiently at her watch. School would be starting in fifteen minutes, but Amanda didn't seem to care. **Perched on** her brand new toy, a shiny white exercise bike with a long giraffe-like neck, she was merrily pedalling away.

"Do you realize how late it is?"

"Can you guess how many calories I've burned?"

"Do you know that German starts in fifteen minutes?"

"Did I tell you that the symbol for calories is a burger and the symbol for speed is a **hare**?" Amanda stared admiringly at the display.

"Do you realize that in future you can walk yourself to school?"

Isy turned round angrily and headed for the door. That girl was a real **liability**. She couldn't be trusted to get anywhere on time.

Lately Amanda had taken to **seasoning** her potato salad, painting her nails, watching the "Cartwrights" on Pro 7 and cutting photos of Prince William out of the newspaper – and all before she left for school! As a

---

to glance – schauen;
to perch on – sitzen auf;
hare – Hase;
liability – Belastung;
to season – würzen

result, they always arrived gasping for breath and bent double with a **stitch**, reaching the door just in time to collide with whichever teacher was taking their class.

"Hey! Wait up!" Amanda **pouted** and slid off the bike. "I didn't even get a chance to see how much I've done!"

She ran into the hallway, grabbed her coat and her bag, and dived after Isy into the lift. They descended in silence. The mirror on the inside of the elevator showed a strong, blonde girl with a big jokey mouth. Her sweaty ponytail featured a **strand** of lilac hair. She was hurriedly buttoning her coat. Next to her was a **dainty** brunette with long **denim-clad** legs and unruly curls that tumbled out of her hair-band. She would have looked pretty, if she hadn't been **determined** to look **outraged**. It wasn't until they walked outside that Isy broke the awkward silence.

"You know, we might still make it, if the lights are green."

Did the lights ever go green when it mattered? It was a chilly morning with a sky that looked like milky glass. They sprinted along one street, then down the next, but just as they reached the **junction**, the lights turned red.

"Well that's that then!" Isy said grimly, turning towards Amanda who, just seconds ago, had been

---

stitch – Seitenstechen;
to pout – schmollen;
strand – Strähne;
dainty – zierlich;
denim-clad – in Jeans;
to be determined – entschlossen sein;
outraged – beleidigt;
junction – Kreuzung

panting alongside her. Her friend wasn't there. She was talking breathlessly into the microphone of a reporter a few metres down the street.

"Over here!" she called out, when she saw Isy looking at them. "Guess what? It's Radio Berlin! They're doing a **moaning**-mike session! You can tell them about anything that's **bugging** you. The programme's live!"

"So what would you like to moan about?" the reporter asked her.

"School!" trumpeted Amanda. Her voice was so loud that Isy could hear it from the crossing. "Especially having to rush like crazy in the morning! I'm calling for flexible start times!"

"In other words, you're saying that the government should be required to reform the school day?" the reporter **probed**, making signals to her colleagues in the van.

"Absolutely!" declared Amanda. Her cheeks were **glowing**.

"And what's your name?"

"Amanda Bornstein! And this is my friend Isolde Schütze!"

But by then Isy had already **grabbed hold of** her arm and was **dragging** her over the crossing.

"Get a move on! The lights have gone green!"

"Hi to the seventh grade!" Amanda shouted over

---

to pant – keuchen, schnaufen;
to moan – meckern, stöhnen;
to bug – nerven;
to probe – nachhaken;
to glow – glühen;
to grab hold of sth – nach etwas greifen;
to drag – ziehen

her shoulder. "And hi to our teacher, Dr Trisch! And to Saskia and Binette, too!"

Then the crossing was behind them and they were already on the final sprint. Gasping for breath, they rushed into the classroom, just as Dr Trisch was handing out their exercise books for dictation.

"Better late than never!" he greeted them sarcastically as they hurried through the door. "Perhaps it's time that we three had a little chat about punctuality. I'm sure you won't mind staying behind over lunchtime?"

"But it's not our fault!" Amanda said breathlessly. She **clutched** her ribs. "We … had … to … stop. I … had … to be … *interviewed*!"

Some of the class began to giggle.

"It's true," Isy backed her up. "Radio Berlin had set up a moaning-mike. They wanted to interview Amanda."

Now the whole class was laughing – with the exception of Dr Trisch. At least he looked interested though. "Really? And what did you decide to moan about?"

"She said *hi* to everyone!" said Isy. Well, that much was true. She sat down at her desk where her exercise book was waiting for her. Amanda had to make her way two rows further back, to her place next to green-haired Saskia, where she'd been sitting ever since the end of the Christmas holidays. Trischi had separated her from Isy **on account of** their continual chatter. Hopefully Amanda would be smart enough to keep her mouth shut and not start on her favourite topic: flexible school hours.

---

to clutch sth – gegen etwas pressen;
on account of – aufgrund von

Amanda had joined their class three years ago when her family moved from Nuremberg to East Berlin. Since then everyone had witnessed how **pigheaded** she could be.

Unfortunately, she seemed **oblivious** to Isy's fears. Nothing and no one could prevent her from starting an educational revolution that day. In no time she had announced her manifesto and could proudly congratulate herself on reducing the whole of 7b to **utter** silence.

Flexible school hours? Was that Amanda's idea of a joke? How on earth would that work?

"There's a school in Berlin that's introduced a flexible school-start already!" proclaimed Amanda. "I read it in the paper. Besides, American doctors have said that it's bad for you to start school before nine. It's all to do with sleeping hormones or something."

She dropped down onto her chair, pleased that she had created such a **stir**. There was no **denying** it: the **entire** class had come alive. Was there really a school with flexible hours? And if so, why had that loud-mouthed **roly-poly** from Nuremberg heard about it first? And anyway, what on earth were sleeping hormones?

Gradually, the new school day began to take shape in the imagination of 7b. Staying in bed until mid-

---

pigheaded – stur;
oblivious – ahnungslos;
utter – absolut;
stir – Aufruhr;
to deny – leugnen;
entire – ganz;
roly-poly – Pummel;
gradually – nach und nach

morning. Watching breakfast television instead of wolfing down their toast and rushing to get to school. It was obvious really: early starts simply had to be bad for you!

After the lesson's turbulent start it was clear that certain pupils would keep firing off new questions in the hope of putting an end to the dictation before it had begun. So much the better, thought Isy. Dictation was never any fun.

Dr Trisch was fully aware of the danger. Jumping in first, he declared that the school system was undoubtedly in need of a change. However, in order to establish whether flexible school hours were a practical option, they would have to learn from the experience of schools that had tried the experiment already.

"In any case, we've already given the matter a good deal of thought. All I can say for the moment is that big changes are **afoot**. In fact, they may come sooner than expected – next week, in fact!" Having made this mysterious pronouncement, he **cast** an **anxious** glance at his watch. "And now, ladies and gentlemen, if I could ask you to open your books!"

Six or so index fingers were already waving in the air. Everyone was suddenly desperate to ask a question.

"I bet it's a school newspaper! That's right, isn't it? We've been asking for one for ages!"

"We're not finally going to get a **drinks dispenser**, are we?"

"Are you going to let us bring our pets to school?"

---

to be afoot – bevorstehen;
to cast – werfen;
anxious – besorgt;
drinks dispenser – Getränkeautomat

In the end, Reginald Häuser, who came from a musical family and whose nickname, Tannhäuser, reflected his love of Wagnerian opera, came out with a suggestion that really **took the biscuit**.

"I've got it!" he exclaimed. "From next week onwards we'll all be **on first-name terms**!"

"I've been calling you by your first-names for years," said Dr Trisch, sounding **bewildered**. "What do you mean?" Then he caught on and seemed to realize that it wasn't his day. He watched his beloved class in silence. Oh, how easy it was to see through their manoeuvres!

He decided to devote what **remained** of the ruined lesson to a discussion of new ways of learning. To start things off, he explained that just as in any other school in the world, some teachers were in favour of the use of computers in classrooms while others opposed it. Computers kept pupils chained to their desks, got in the way of their natural freedom of movement and robbed them of their creativity, some argued. Others pointed out that young people had to learn to think using complex systems, otherwise they would never be able to solve the world's problems. But there was one thing that everyone agreed on: if a country wanted to compete on an international level, it had to train its citizens *before* they started work in its factories or laboratories.

"It all starts in the classroom!" their teacher announced. "The world's sum total of knowledge – the

---

to take the biscuit – dem Ganzen die Krone aufsetzen;
to be on first-name terms – sich duzen;
bewildered – verblüfft;
to remain – übrig bleiben

sum of all the information that we possess – is increasing at an incredible rate. Experts **estimate** that it's doubling every five years!"

He paused for effect before continuing, "A new culture of learning is **emerging**, and at this school you'll be among the first to profit from it."

If what he was saying was true, they were fantastically lucky. By the start of the next school year the school would have its own state-of-the-art computer room, as well as Internet contact with an American school. At night their electronic mail boxes would fill up with information sent from faraway America or elsewhere in Europe, allowing pupils from both **hemispheres** to communicate with each other.

Trischi twisted his head in his **polo-neck jumper** like a black **bird of prey**. He watched them in anticipation as though waiting for a sign of excitement. Polo-necks were his favourite type of sweater, although according to some of the girls, he only wore them because they covered up **hickeys**.

"Of course, the language of computing is English, and our partner school is in Philadelphia!" he finished off.

He was instantly confronted with a **barrage** of questions. Most of the class simply wanted to know where Philadelphia was. As far as Isy could see, they were all excited by the news – especially Amanda, who had her

---

to estimate – schätzen;
to emerge – entstehen;
hemisphere – Erdteil;
polo-neck jumper – Rollkragenpullover;
bird of prey – Raubvogel;
hickey – Knutschfleck;
barrage – Schwall

own PC and was really good at English anyway. From her point of view, things couldn't be better.

Once Trischi had finished explaining that Philadelphia was the capital of New Jersey, on the east coast of America, he announced that the school would be organizing a competition to mark the **launch** of the Internet project. The aim was to work in small groups and **compile** a web report that would introduce American schoolkids to specific places in Berlin. They could choose the location and use pictures and words. The best report would be uploaded onto the Internet at the beginning of the new school year, when the Internet connection would be opened **ceremoniously**.

"Remember to look at the notice-board next week," their teacher encouraged them. "You'll find all the details, including the maximum word count and the deadline for **submission**. And, of course, you'll be able to read all about the prize."

What? There was going to be a prize as well? The whole class started talking excitedly, but just then the bell rang for the end of the lesson and Dr Trisch raised his hand to **quieten** them **down**.

"That's enough now! You won't get another word out of me. You'll have to wait until next week."

---

launch – Start;
to compile – erstellen;
ceremonious – feierlich;
submission – Abgabe;
to quieten sb down – jmdn. beruhigen

– 2 –

On Monday the details appeared on the notice-board. Participation was **voluntary**. The web report had to be submitted by the end of May. First prize was a trip to a computer centre in Philadelphia!

"Philadelphia!" whispered Amanda. Her eyes shone with enthusiasm in the dim light of the corridor. "Just think: you and me in the States! That would be dreamy!"

It would be better than that, thought Isy. It would be out of this world!

A crowd of pupils had **gathered** in front of the notice-board, and soon Berlin was being **sliced up** like a cake. Each group wanted the tastiest portion for itself. They practically **came to blows** over the Brandenburg Gate, the Victory Column, the Globe Fountain and the television tower. Saskia and Binette **plumped for** the Fairy Tale Fountain in Friedrichshain, Richard and Holger settled on the television tower, and Tannhäuser mumbled something about the State Opera belonging to him.

"We'll have the zoo!" cried Isy before yet another tasty **morsel** was seized from under their noses. "Amanda and I will take the zoological gardens!"

---

voluntary – freiwillig; to gather – versammeln;
to slice up – aufteilen;
to come to blows – sich streiten;
to plump for – sich entscheiden für;
morsel – Bissen

"Why on earth would we want the zoo?" whined Amanda. "We'll take the castle instead!"

"But I don't want the castle!"

"And I don't want the zoo!"

"Then take your **precious** castle!" Isy said **crossly**. "I'm perfectly capable of doing the zoo on my own!"

The final lesson of the day was sport. Fifteen minutes later they were sitting together in the train, heading for the zoo. Isy had always known that her friend would join her in the end. Amanda didn't really have any objection to the zoo. Her only objection was to being **bossed around**. Isy sometimes jumped in before Amanda had a chance to speak. But what else should she have done? If she hadn't spoken up quickly, someone else would have stolen the zoo!

"What do you say we call on the director and tell him about the project? We'll need some kind of special pass, so we don't have to **stump up** three Euros every time we go in."

The city's zoo already had special rates for Berlin's schoolkids, but the cost was **bound to** add up in the course of the project.

Amanda nodded distractedly. She'd **purchased** a copy of her favourite magazine from the kiosk, and was reading the latest news on the English royal family. Prince William was her **current heartthrob**,

---

precious – wertvoll;
cross – sauer, ärgerlich;
to boss around – herumschubsen;
to stump up – löhnen;
to be bound to – müssen;
to purchase – kaufen;
current – aktuell;
heartthrob – Schwarm

and there was even a picture of him hanging over her bed.

At first Isy had been **baffled** by Amanda's interest in royal gossip. Back in the **GDR**, the only queens had been queen bees. To her mind, princes and princesses belonged to fairytales.

She **peered** inquisitively through the fogged-up windows. It had been **drizzling** since first thing that morning, and the streets and the roofs shone damply with water. The silhouette of the Victory Column faded from view. After a while the trees and bushes of the zoological gardens appeared to be closing in on the elegant boulevards. Isy tapped her friend on the shoulder. "Time to get out!"

Amanda always **pretended** not to be impressed by Zoo Station. According to her it was nothing compared with Manhattan. Even so, the roaring traffic and the crowds of people always took their breath away. Besides, Amanda had never actually been to New York, she only knew about it from her dad.

"Elephant gate or lion gate?" asked Isy during their short walk to the zoo. They opted for elephant gate. It was closer to the aquarium.

"We want to see the director!" Isy informed the grey-haired lady at the counter. She **squinted at** them through the pane of glass.

"Do you have an appointment?"

They shook their heads in silence.

---

baffled – verblüfft;
GDR – DDR;
to peer – spähen;
to drizzle – regnen;
to pretend – vortäuschen;
to squint at sb/sth – einen Blick auf jmdn./etwas werfen

"Well, you'll have to make one!" She **charged** them the reduced rate for schoolkids, and pushed their admission tickets through the **hatch**. Their project was in danger of becoming expensive.

"We should have gone for Charlottenburg Castle instead," **insisted** Amanda. "Think how much this will cost us!"

"Tickets to your beloved castle wouldn't be any cheaper! Let's talk to Trischi. The school will have to apply for special passes for us," said Isy.

They sniffed the fresh air in contentment. It wasn't even spring yet, and on a rainy day like today the zoo's few visitors were evidently **diehard** fans. Even the animals had **made themselves scarce**. Isy spotted antelopes grazing in their enclosures. There was a little lake nearby, and at its centre an island whose **banks** were lined with **willows**. In the summer months the trees **trailed** their **leafy mane** of branches through the water, while flamingos brightened the scene with pink dots of colour. At this time of year though, it was too cold for them to be outside.

"Why don't we start by making a list of all the animals that seem interesting," suggested Isy. "We can choose which ones we want to write about later."

"And who's going to write them down?"

---

to charge – berechnen;
hatch – Schalter;
to insist – beharren;
diehard – eingefleischt;
to make oneself scarce – sich rar machen;
bank – Ufer;
willow – Trauerweide;
to trail – hier: hängen lassen;
leafy mane – Mähne aus Blättern

"You are! Besides, you'll have to type it all up on your computer when we get home."

"Why does it always have to be me?" Amanda gave a **groan**. "By the way, have you remembered to ask your parents about that language course yet? If we don't sign up soon, we won't get a place."

There wasn't much point even asking, thought Isy. The **taster course** for beginners' English was far too expensive. Maybe her family would be able to **afford** such luxuries when her mum found a job. In the meantime Amanda would have to make the trip alone.

Her friend still had to make up for the last time she went to London. Last year she had accompanied her dad on a one-day trip to the English capital. While Mr Bornstein was in a conference, Amanda had rushed off on her own. Her aim had been to find the Queen or some other member of the royal family to shake hands with. Unfortunately for her, the taxi driver hadn't understood what she was saying, and rather than taking her to Buckingham Palace, he'd dropped her at the Bank of England instead. She was determined not to let that happen again …

"How about a language course in Philadelphia?" said Isy. "That would be **heaps** more fun, and it won't cost a cent!"

"Who says we're going to win?" Amanda looked surprised at the thought of it.

By now they'd arrived at the aquarium, a famous historic building in which Berlin Zoo kept its fish,

---

groan – Stöhnen;
taster course – Schnupperkurs;
to afford – sich leisten;
heap – Haufen

amphibians and reptiles. They slipped through the doors, together with a group of Japanese tourists who were talking excitedly amongst themselves. At least it was warm in there.

Carefully studying the labels, they wandered past the panes of glass that stretched up to the ceiling, gazing at **shoals** of **darting** fish. **Carp** and slow-moving **catfish** swam by, followed by **plaice** too large to fit in any frying pan. The view changed with each new tank: white **jellyfish** floated through the silent world of water, sea anemones looked like graceful **tulle hoops**, and an enormous **red grouper** resembled a biblical monster.

Isy loved the green-tinged light of the aquarium. Even the noises seemed strangely **muffled**. It almost seemed like a dream.

The other visitors seemed to find the aquarium restful, too. Most of them were sitting contentedly on benches, reading or **knitting**, just like the old lady with the grey **bun** and pink glasses who advised Amanda not to leave her **holdall** lying around unsupervised.

---

shoal – Schwarm;
to dart – sausen, flitzen;
carp – Karpfen;
catfish – Wels;
plaice – Scholle;
jellyfish – Qualle;
tulle – Tüll;
hoop – Ring, Reifen;
red grouper – Zackenbarsch;
muffled – gedämpft;
to knit – stricken;
bun – Dutt;
holdall – Sporttasche

"You ought to keep an eye on your things, you know," she said. Her voice sounded surprisingly youthful. "Not everyone is as honest as they seem."

The old woman was right. Amanda hesitated, then picked up the **burdensome** bag, and they continued past brightly coloured tropical fish whose exotic names were dutifully noted by Amanda. The next tank was full of **petal**-like coral formations and filigree sea-horses. She wrote down the details. There were some funny-looking creatures, too, like the American **paddlefish** with its elongated sword-shaped nose that Amanda thought would be great for **pricking** potatoes.

But the highlight of the visit was the **whitetip shark**, a truly impressive **specimen**. Maybe Isy would have been able to admire it more freely, if it hadn't reminded her of the great white shark in *Jaws*. Amanda shuddered to look at it, too.

Standing next to them by the shark tank was a group of **Goths**, dressed entirely in black leather. The only girl among them looked totally cool. Her pretty face was painted the colour of chalk, and her black-rimmed eyes twinkled to match the black lipstick of her smile. At school there were **rumours** about Goths hanging out in graveyards and **vaults**. According to some people, they decorated their homes with black candles and **skulls**, and a few of them even slept in **coffins**.

---

burdensome – lästig;
petal – Blüte;
paddlefish – Löffelstör;
to prick – hier: wenden;
whitetip shark – Weißflossenhai;
specimen – Exemplar; Goth – Grufti;
rumour – Gerücht; vault – Gewölbe;
skull – Totenschädel; coffin – Sarg

Isy didn't actually believe the rumours, but they were pleasantly spooky. Amanda watched the Goths in fascination. It was unusual to see them by daylight in their distinctive black outfits.

"Cool clothes," she whispered admiringly.

One of the Goths, a tall guy with a blond **Mohican** by the name of Paul, was trying to get the others to say cheese. He pulled out his camera.

"How about fish instead?" called the girl, and so they all yelled "Fish!"

"I'll be back in a second," said Isy and walked along the silent corridor of water to the entrance, where she found the door to the WC.

By the time she got back to Amanda, the Goths had moved on. Amanda was keen to go home as well. She **claimed** that she would never be able to eat fish again if they stayed any longer at the aquarium.

Isy agreed that they could leave. They'd seen enough for an **initial** visit.

"That was **fab**!" she said happily, **taking stock of** their day. They were waiting on the crowded platform for the train to take them home.

"Fab?" growled Amanda. "What's fab about being bored? What are you planning on telling the kids in Philadelphia? Romantic stories about paddlefish?"

Uh-oh. Surely Amanda wasn't still hung up on the castle? Just as Isy was about to tell her that there were at least another hundred thousand types of animals in the zoo besides paddlefish, Amanda let out a sudden **squeal**.

---

mohican - Irokesenschnitt; to claim – behaupten;
initial – erste(r); fab – super;
to take stock of – Bilanz ziehen aus
squeal – Schrei

"Look! My bag! It just moved!" She directed a trembling finger at the holdall that was lying between them. Isy looked at the bag **in bewilderment**.

"Are you **nuts**?"

"I'm telling you, it just moved!" her friend repeated **stubbornly** and pulled back the zip.

The next second something dark and **furry** shot out of the bag and clung on to her. It seemed as though the trip to the zoo hadn't been quite as uneventful as Amanda had claimed.

---

in bewilderment – verblüfft;
to be nuts – verrückt sein;
stubborn – störrisch;
furry – haarig

– 3 –

Something huge happened to Amanda today," said Isy, breathing in the warm smell of bacon at the dinner table. "I don't suppose any of you have ever found a monkey in your bag!"

She paused for a moment, enjoying her family's astonishment, then proceeded to recount everything that had happened that day, starting with the details of the prize on the notice-board and finishing with the moment when Amanda had found herself holding a monkey in her arms.

"She got the **fright** of her life, you know. It even made me jump, too! You should have seen it!"

"I guess it must have climbed into her bag," said her mother, who always had a practical answer for everything. "Had you been to the monkey house?"

"No! We were in the aquarium. Logically speaking, it should have been a fish. In any case, it wasn't Amanda's bag." Isy sighed. "We didn't notice at first. Amanda's bag was navy blue and the other bag was black. Now she's lost all her sports kit – expensive stuff from Nike."

"She must have taken the wrong bag then! An easy mistake," said her father. Benedikt rushed to agree with him, "It's the obvious explanation. I bet they were talking about boys again!" He held up his hands and **mim-**

---

fright – Schrecken;
to mimick – nachahmen

icked two ducks in an imaginary conversation. "They were too busy chatting to notice."

"Of course, we weren't talking about boys! We've got better things to do, you know. We were working on an **assignment**, actually," Isy said in a **dignified** voice. "And anyway, Amanda never took her eyes off the holdall. We carried it around everywhere. An old woman told us to be careful, so we took her advice!"

"Well, one of you must be getting forgetful then," Benedikt **muttered scornfully**. The conversation turned back to their mother's search for work. She didn't want to work with computers, but the job she'd been offered last week required her to do so. Benedikt was trying hard to change her mind. It was obvious that he'd spotted an **opportunity** for them to get a computer at last. Until now their parents had always had more urgent things to spend their money on.

All Isy wanted was to tell them the rest of the story. She and Amanda had carried the monkey home inside the bag. In the end, they'd decided not to take it straight back to the zoo. After all, it hadn't necessarily come from there **in the first place**. And how were they going to explain why they were carrying a monkey in a bag that didn't even belong to them? Eventually Amanda had taken it upstairs and pretended to her parents that it had come in from the balcony. But evidently Isy's family weren't interested in hearing the story.

---

assignment – Beitrag;
dignified – würdevoll;
to mutter – murmeln;
scornful – verächtlich;
opportunity – Gelegenheit;
in the first place – in erster Linie/überhaupt

Her parents weren't especially **fond of** Amanda anyway. In their eyes she was a **spoiled** West German who encouraged their daughter to have unreasonable expectations. The truth was, it was nothing to do with Amanda. Everyone in Isy's class wanted clothes with trendy logos on them. Why couldn't grown-ups understand that cool clothes made you feel cool about life? They made you feel like you **belonged**. Her parents were **kidding themselves** if they couldn't see that.

Isy disappeared up to her bedroom in disappointment. It was the smallest room in the apartment, little more than a cupboard, but at least it was hers. Before she settled down, she stopped to greet Selma, who was **curled up** on her patchwork quilt, **purring** contentedly. Then she sat down at her desk, which was home to some books, two porcelain cats, a half-eaten chocolate egg and a photo of Granny Dora – plus a plump yellow **primrose** that had been left over from their pot-planting session on the balcony the weekend before. It was amazing how the little flowers spread their **cheer** throughout the room. Maybe she should give the primrose a name. Paula would be perfect! Amanda had a **pet cactus** that she **referred to** as Aeschylus. She took it everywhere, even when she went on holiday. The prickly globetrotter had started

---

to be fond of – begeistert sein;
spoiled – verzogen;
to belong – hier: dazugehören;
to be kidding oneself – sich etwas vormachen;
curled up – zusammengerollt;
to purr – schnurren;
primrose – Primel;
cheer – gute Laune; pet cactus – Lieblingskaktus;
to refer to – sich beziehen auf

life in West Germany and had seen far more of the world than Isy had so far.

She opened her books to make a start on her homework. She was trying hard to concentrate, but despite her best efforts, it just wouldn't work. Her thoughts were like inquisitive **puppy dogs** – they kept sniffing at the mysterious holdall.

How on earth had the bags been mixed up? Was Benedikt right? Had Amanda been **distracted** for a moment? The longer Isy thought about it, the more convinced she felt that Amanda had overlooked a **crucial** fact. It probably hadn't seemed important at the time. Sometimes the most trivial details were the key to the mystery. That was one thing that Isy had learnt from all those detective novels that she'd read.

But it was **weird** that she hadn't seen anything herself, even though she'd been there all along. Why hadn't she noticed that the bags had been swapped? Isy started to work half-heartedly on the first maths question. Had she really been there all along? No! That wasn't entirely true! She had almost forgotten that Amanda had been on her own for a couple of minutes. A couple of minutes in which Isy hadn't been able to watch over Amanda or the bag!

Isy exploded into action. She ran down the hallway to phone her friend. From the kitchen she could hear that her parents were shouting. Ever since Isy's mum had lost her job, they had been arguing continually. It was mainly about money. As an engineer Isy's mum

---

puppy dog – Hundebaby;
to be distracted – abgelenkt sein;
crucial – entscheidend;
weird – merkwürdig

had earned a good **salary** in the GDR, and she wasn't **accustomed to** counting every cent. Isy could see that it must be awful having to fight with her dad over every single bill. I'll never get married, she promised herself. At long last Amanda answered the phone.

"You've got to think hard!" Isy told her. "Tell me exactly what happened whilst I was in the toilet."

"Isy! That monkey's just squeezed toothpaste all over my dad!"

Then Amanda finally seemed to understand the question. "What do you mean? Nothing happened at all!"

"Did you let the bag out of your sight?"

"How many times do I have to tell you? No!"

"Something must have happened," Isy pressed her. "Something you've forgotten."

"Oh no, now it's hanging off the **curtain rail**!" Amanda groaned.

"Think back to the Goths! When did they leave? They'd left by the time I got back."

"The Goths? They **cleared off** as soon as I'd taken their picture."

"What? You took a picture of them?"

"Is that a problem? They wanted a photo of the whole group, that's all."

"But you never told me!"

Amanda sighed impatiently. "I don't see why it's so important."

There was a pause. "Amanda!" said Isy in a shocked voice. "Your stupidity leaves me speechless! What do

---

salary – Gehalt; to be accustomed to – gewöhnt sein an;
curtain rail – Gardinenstange;
to clear off – abhauen

you mean, you never lost sight of the bag? How can anyone look through a viewfinder whilst watching their bag? Do you realize that you left that bag unsupervised for at least ten seconds? I'd say that's important!"

The only answer was the sound of **shattering** glass.

"As you probably heard," said Amanda, "that monkey's just smashed into our **cabinet**!" She slammed down the phone.

Isy hung up, too. Was there any hope for Amanda? She'd forgotten to **mention** the most important fact of all! Luckily, thanks to her own **persistence**, she now knew that one of the Goths could have swapped the two bags. If so, the Goth would now be in possession of Amanda's trendy sports **gear** while she'd been landed with a wild ape. What a bizarre kind of swap! But even more **intriguing** was the question of why anyone would take a monkey to the aquarium in the first place. At this point surely alarm bells would be ringing in the minds of all the detectives she knew from books, films and TV serials. In any case, to Isy the noise seemed **deafening**!

---

to shatter – zerbrechen;
cabinet – Vitrine;
to mention – erwähnen;
persistence – Hartnäckigkeit;
gear – Zeug;
intriguing – merkwürdig;
deafening – ohrenbetäubend

– 4 –

The next morning Amanda turned up punctually at Isy's front door. So **miracles** could happen after all! The trouble was, she looked completely tired out. Her hair was messy, there was a blob of face cream on her right eyebrow, and her talisman, an old-fashioned black-and-white **checked** scarf, had been hurriedly knotted around her neck like a **noose**.

"We have to think of something!" she said before Isy had a chance to comment. "That monkey is a pest! If we're not careful, my mum will have a nervous breakdown. Thank goodness it was quiet overnight. It went to sleep in the **tumble-dryer**. But now it won't let anyone near the bathroom."

"How did you wash?" asked Isy **in astonishment**.

"We had to use the sink in the toilet. Dad left for work without shaving."

"You've got to be strong," Isy told her. "Just hang in there until we've solved the mystery. There's something fishy about this, Amanda. The whole thing stinks!"

"You mean the monkey stinks! It's not even **housetrained**!"

---

miracle – Wunder;
checked – kariert;
noose – Schlinge;
tumble-dryer – Wäschetrockner;
in astonishment – erstaunt;
housetrained – stubenrein

"It's only for a couple more days. We're lucky that you've got such a big flat!"

"But my parents are going mad! They don't understand why the monkey had to come in over *our* balcony and not somebody else's. They want me to take it to an **animal sanctuary** today!"

"I think we should go to a pet shop and find out what kind of monkey it is."

"OK, fine," said Amanda, **relenting**. "Just one more day. But what am I going to tell my parents?"

"Tell them that the sanctuary was full, but it's doing its best to find a home for the monkey. **Appeal to** their love of animals!"

"I've tried that already! I argued with them until I was blue in the face!" Amanda bent down to re-tie her shoelaces. Then they set off.

Soon they reached the little baker's shop. Its door was propped open in all weathers, allowing the mouth-watering smell of freshly baked bread and **sugary buns** to **tempt** the passers-by. Amanda disappeared inside and returned with two doughnuts. She was accompanied by two girls from their class: Saskia, whose **seaweed**-green hair was now **streaked** with blue highlights, and Binette, who had bought a couple of doughnuts, too. Isy noticed Amanda putting a warning finger to her lips while the others weren't looking. She knew exactly what her friend was trying to tell her.

---

animal sanctuary – Tierheim;
to relent – nachgeben;
to appeal to – appellieren an;
sugary bun – süßes Teilchen;
to tempt – in Versuchung führen;
seaweed – Seegras;
streaked – gesträhnt

Amanda didn't want the class to know about the ape. Everyone thought they were **calamity queens** anyway, and it would only make things worse. But there was no denying that strange things happened to them.

There was the time when they'd found a man's body in the woods. The police had arrived to inspect the **corpse**, but by that time he'd recovered from his lunchtime rest and was **harvesting** mushrooms again! That was a school trip that class 7b would never forget. Not all of their adventures ended so badly though. Last autumn they'd **managed to** help solve the mystery of a mail robbery and, in the end, they'd had their pictures in the paper. But being successful didn't always make you popular. Amanda was right. They'd have to solve the problem on their own. Besides, the others would only start coming up with stupid comments like "A Case for Two" or "Murder, She Wrote".

For the first time in ages they didn't have to race to school. **Munching** on their doughnuts, they chatted about what they'd dreamt that night. They even arrived on time!

Amanda's sleep had been interrupted by a **nightmare**: a famous chat-show host had invited her onto his TV show so she could demonstrate how to cook a good meal. But as the spotlight turned to her, her mind went blank. She was standing in front of the oven in the famous TV kitchen, and couldn't remember what the recipe had said!

---

calamity queen – hier: Katastrophenweib;
corpse – Leiche;
to harvest – ernten, pflücken;
to manage to do sth – es schaffen, etwas zu tun;
to munch – kauen;
nightmare – Alptraum

"It was *sooo* embarrassing," moaned Amanda, who'd started cooking for fun last autumn. "The whole class was watching!"

"Well, I wasn't," Sassi assured her. "I was asleep!" They all laughed. Binette wanted to know what kind of meal she'd been planning.

"A candlelit dinner!" explained Amanda. "A romantic dinner with candles and everything."

"You get them in old detective stories," said Isy with a grin. "That's when the murderer is usually **revealed**!"

That morning they had to sit patiently through one **period** of Maths and one period of Music, followed by two periods of English and finally History. Afterwards they went back to the Bornsteins' apartment to take a Polaroid picture of Amanda's new flatmate. They showed the photo to the shopkeeper at the pet store.

"Can you tell us what kind of monkey this is?"

While Amanda **took charge of** the conversation, Isy sniffed the air. It smelt of bird feed, **grit** and dog biscuits – a smell that seemed to **waft** through every pet store.

The shopkeeper examined the picture closely. "**Well, I never!** A brown **capuchin monkey**! Is it yours?"

Amanda glanced helplessly at Isy.

"My friend just **inherited** it!" Isy cut in.

"Her grandfather was a … a big game hunter!"

---

to reveal – entdecken, aufdecken;
period – Unterrichtsstunde;
to take charge of sth – sich um etwas kümmern;
grit – Vogelsand; to waft – schweben;
Well, I never! – Sieh an!;
capuchin monkey – Kapuzineraffe;
to inherit – erben

The shopkeeper peered over his **rimless** spectacles at them, staring at Isy, then Amanda, then the photo. He seemed to sense that something was wrong.

"Are you planning to sell it?"

"Err, no. Is it **valuable**?"

"Brown capuchins come from South America. They're a protected **species**. No one's allowed to export them. You'd be looking at a collector's price – and that varies, of course."

"Just give us a **rough** idea," Amanda encouraged him. She was practically bursting with curiosity.

"Well, I'd say you'd probably get ten thousand euros."

Ten thousand euros? They stared at the shopkeeper as though he'd already handed them the money. Out of the corner of her eye Isy saw that her friend had almost forgotten to breathe. Amanda stuffed the photo back into her jacket pocket and thanked the man for his help.

Just as they were leaving the store, the shopkeeper called out after them, "You know, the last time I saw a handsome little fellow like that was in the zoo!"

The two friends almost fell over as they hurried through the door.

"My granddad's still alive, thank you very much!" Amanda announced with a grin once they were far enough away. "Big game hunting, I ask you! He's an **accountant**, just like my dad!" She grabbed hold of Isy's arm. "Did you hear what he said? Ten thousand Euros for one little monkey! How crazy is that?"

---

rimless – randlos;
valuable – wertvoll;
species – Tierart;
rough – ungefähr;
accountant – Steuerberater

Isy was shaking her head **incredulously**. "I can't believe it! That Goth must have had the shock of his life when he realized he'd picked up your bag!"

"You bet he did!"

For a moment they walked on in silence, each busy with their thoughts. Then Amanda suddenly whispered, "Hey, Isolde, we're rich!"

"What do you mean, *we're* rich?"

"Well, it's our monkey now!" Amanda gave the photo in her pocket a knowing pat. "Don't look at me like that! We've hit the jackpot!"

"But it doesn't belong to us!" Isy was staring at Amanda as though she'd just suggested that they should rob the city bank. Their **pace** had slowed over the past few metres. They came to a halt in front of a little travel agency that was advertising this season's special deal: an Easter trip to see the pyramids in Egypt. Ever since last week the front window had been filled with a **lurid** green plastic palm tree and a life-size camel. It looked surprisingly real.

"Well, if it's not ours, whose is it?" Amanda asked **innocently**.

"Don't be ridiculous: it belongs to the Goth!"

"But we don't know his address."

"So what? That doesn't mean we can sell his monkey!"

"Well, he took my stuff, remember! Nike's expensive, you know."

"Pink sports kit – I'm sure it **made his day**!"

---

incredulous – ungläubig;
pace – Schritt;
lurid – grell;
innocent – unschuldig;
to make one's day – jmdm. den Tag retten

Amanda chewed her lower lip. She looked as though she was about to cry. Then she threw back her head **defiantly**. "We could use the money for the English course in London. Next year we could even go to France – or maybe Italy! We could go wherever you wanted. And we'd even be able to buy ourselves some brand new clothes. This is the opportunity of a lifetime!"

"That's all very well," said Isy, "but selling other people's stuff is seriously uncool. You can count me out!"

"In that case, I'll sell it by myself!" her friend **hissed** back.

"That's just the kind of **behaviour** I'd expect from you, Amanda!"

"But the monkey was in my bag! You can't argue with that! In fact, technically, the monkey belongs to me!"

"*Your* bag? I don't think so!"

"Now look who's behaving like a stupid East German!"

"Well, you're behaving like a spoiled West German!"

Why was Amanda bringing up that East versus West rubbish? They **barely** knew anything about the wall except what their parents had told them. After all, Germany had been reunified by the time they'd started school – Amanda in Nuremberg and Isy in East Berlin. When they were little, they would never have guessed

---

defiant – trotzig;
to hiss – zischen;
behaviour – Verhalten;
barely – kaum

that there were two German heads of state – they were more interested in the Little Sandman on TV. Amanda's shelves had been filled with books translated from Swedish and Italian, while Isy's children stories came from Russia and Hungary. Even now Isy still sometimes used East German words for things like supermarkets and sausages. But what did any of that have to do with the monkey? Never before in their four years of friendship had they stared at each other so angrily.

Just then they heard the noise of an **engine** as a burgundy Golf pulled up alongside them. A man with thinning hair and a small moustache leaned out of the car.

"Well, we meet again!" he said with a **chuckle**. "How are you both?"

Now that was a surprise. The cloud of **hostility** that was separating the two friends suddenly lifted.

"Thank goodness you're here, Mr Rimpau!" Isy exclaimed **in relief**. "We've got a problem."

---

engine – Motor;
chuckle – Kichern;
hostility – Feindseligkeit;
in relief – erleichtert

– 5 –

Mr Rimpau had first appeared on the scene during the autumn holidays last year. He wasn't **merely** a friend though: he wrote crime novels for a living and was a famous author. Isy and Amanda had met him and his cute dog Alfredo last October in Altgrünheide when they'd arrived before the rest of their class at their field centre in Brandenburg. The centre had just been renovated, but it needed a really good clean. Lots of mothers had offered their help, but one by one they'd all dropped out, leaving only Isy's mum, who'd been determined to keep her promise. Then the day before she was **due to** start cleaning, she'd fallen over Selma and broken her leg – a misfortune which caused her to lose her job and nearly cost 7b their long-awaited field trip. It had already been **postponed** once before, and now it seemed as though they wouldn't be able to find a cleaner.

That same night Isy had found herself dreaming the most incredible dream. It convinced her that she and Amanda should take action themselves. As a result, they'd spent the most exciting week of their lives in a spooky old **lodge** in the forest.

Mr Rimpau had been living in a **rented** summer-

---

merely – nur;
to be due to – sollen, müssen;
to postpone – verschieben;
lodge – Forsthaus;
to rent – mieten

house nearby, where he was focusing on his work. In spite of a few misunderstandings and mix-ups, he'd soon proved to be a **dependable** friend and **ally**.

"I hope it isn't anything too disastrous," said Mr Rimpau, glancing quickly at his watch. "I have to get to the airport!"

"Not yet, it isn't," Isy reassured him, hurriedly filling him in on the details of their assignment and the events of the day before.

"I know we're always getting into trouble," she said self-critically, "but we've never had a problem with a monkey before! What do you think we should do?"

It was obvious that Mr Rimpau would like nothing better than to lean back in his armchair in Altgrünheide with a pipe in his mouth, **reflecting on** what he'd heard. But that wasn't an option. He didn't even have time to go for a quick hot chocolate with them. The aeroplane was waiting to take him to Munich.

"Have you called the zoo yet? Maybe someone's handed in your holdall and left a note with their address. That would solve the problem!" he said.

The two girls exchanged a look of embarrassment. They hadn't even thought of that! Sometimes the simplest solution was the most difficult to find.

"But what if the Goth can't remember where he lost his bag?" said Isy, **concerned**.

"Who knows if he even lives in Berlin? Perhaps he didn't notice the mix-up until he was on his way home to Dessau or Bochum or wherever," the author said thoughtfully.

---

dependable – verlässlich;
ally – Verbündeter;
to reflect on – nachdenken über;
in concern – besorgt

For a moment there was a helpless silence.

"Well, keep your chins up!" said Mr Rimpau full of optimism. "You should start by asking at the zoo, and if they don't know anything about it, you should look in the papers. Maybe someone will have placed an advertisement. And if all else **fails** – you'll know where to find me!"

He opened the **car boot** and pressed a slim book into each girl's hands. It was his latest novel. *One Murder Too Many at the Zoo*. What a coincidence! As he climbed back into his Golf, a warm smell of tobacco and leather wafted out of the car, reminding Isy of Altgrünheide. Then Mr Rimpau joined the roaring traffic in the direction of Tegel airport.

They waved after him, but a troop of rollerbladers was skating towards them, and they suddenly had to **dodge**. Isy always felt proud to have such a famous person as her friend. Amanda looked **starry-eyed**, too.

They went in search of a telephone box and **punched in** the number of the zoo. Amanda's holdall hadn't turned up, and no one had left her a message.

"Don't go getting your hopes up!" Isy told her friend when she noticed her ten-thousand-euro smile.

"I don't give up that easily, you know. There's always tomorrow!"

The next morning it was Amanda's turn to wait for Isy. It was so unusual for Isy to be late that Amanda had already started worrying about her by the time she appeared around the corner.

---

to fail – schief gehen;
car boot – Kofferraum;
to dodge – ausweichen;
starry-eyed – verklärt;
to punch in – hier: wählen

"I thought you must be ill or something," she greeted Isy in relief, then started to complain about the monkey.

"It ate our miniature palm tree and then **swallowed** our philodendron for dessert. We'd grown that plant from **seed**!"

"Maybe you need to feed it more vegetables," suggested Isy. She'd spent half the night **devouring** Mr Rimpau's new novel and had barely made it out of bed this morning.

"I don't have to feed it anything at all!" Amanda said crossly. "Besides, it **tore open** my parents' pillows and **clogged** the toilet with beans!" Amanda took a deep breath. "We've got to sell that creature, Isy!"

"Forget it!"

"But why not? I hope you don't think I'd take more than my fair share. I'll split every single euro with you!"

"It's got nothing to do with that."

"Then stop being such a goody-goody! You know as well as I do that it hasn't been reported missing. We can't return it because we don't know who it belongs to!" Amanda **swelled** like a fighting **cock**. "Tell me what the problem is, or I'm taking it straight to the pet store!"

"I will tell you – just as soon as we're on the train."

"Which train?"

---

to swallow – schlucken, hier: fressen;
seed – Samen;
to devour – verschlingen;
to tear open – aufreißen;
to clog – verstopfen;
to swell – hier: sich aufplustern;
cock – Hahn

"The train to the zoo!"

"What? Not the zoo again! Can't we do something else, you know, like shopping, swimming or skating – or the movies?"

"Right now the zoo is more important."

Amanda didn't know that Isy's bedtime reading had opened her eyes to the truth. It had given her **goose-bumps**! Mr Rimpau had written a terrifying thriller that proved that the goings-on at the zoo probably weren't as harmless as they seemed. Isy couldn't wait to tell Amanda everything she knew, but she didn't want to get her worried too soon. There was a strong chance that she'd simply **freak out**. Isy decided to wait until they were on the train, their long legs stretched **casually** in front of them. Both pairs of jeans ended in identical pairs of trendy trainers.

While the train proceeded through the various stations, Isy told the **unsuspecting** Amanda about the meaning of "contract crime": a type of crime that **involved** rich clients paying for **goods** that criminals would **obtain** using whatever means proved necessary. Sometimes rare animals were stolen.

Of course, it was all news to Amanda. She didn't take any interest in that kind of thing. Her heart belonged to love stories, romantic pop-songs, the Kelly Family, Prince William, the Queen and delicious new recipes.

---

goose-bumps – Gänsehaut;
to freak out – ausflippen;
casual – lässig;
unsuspecting – ahnungslos;
to involve – einbeziehen;
goods – Waren;
to obtain – beschaffen

"Why are you telling me all this?" she enquired **suspiciously**.

"Because it's exactly the kind of mess we're muddled up in!"

Amanda removed her chewing-gum in surprise. "Are you completely nuts?"

"Well, think about it! Didn't I say it was weird that someone was carrying around a monkey in the zoo?" Isy looked around **warily**, but the small group of passengers in the compartment were reading the newspaper or staring out of the window. The punk sitting diagonally opposite them had lowered his pink Mohican and was **scraping** the dirt from his nails.

She continued in a whisper, "Amanda, you know how valuable that creature is! Just imagine for a second that it had been stolen from the zoo for someone with heaps of money. The mafia are **involved with** that kind of thing! Just think: you probably walked off with the criminal's bag! Maybe that's why no one has reported it to the zoo!"

"I may have what?" Amanda was almost speechless. "Why do you always come up with such stupid ideas?"

"Stupid? Don't make me laugh! The mafia exists, you know. If you don't believe me, read *One Murder Too Many at the Zoo*! It's about a mad old lady who's **got a thing about** cats and desperately wants a white tiger for her house – like those tigers in Las Vegas that work with Siegfried and Roy!"

---

suspicious – misstrauisch;
wary – vorsichtig, misstrauisch;
to scrape – kratzen;
to be involved with – zu tun haben mit;
to have got a thing about sth – vernarrt sein in

"Oh, I get it!" Amanda interrupted. She sounded relieved. "Mr Rimpau **made** it all **up**."

"Made it up? These are facts!" Isy leaned closer to Amanda's ear. "That's why we've got to check out the monkey house. Maybe they haven't even noticed that a monkey's gone missing!"

The monkey house wasn't far from the elephant gate where they proudly presented the special passes that their teacher had obtained for them. Unlike the famous aquarium, the monkey house was a brand new building. Tree **stumps**, leaves, shiny metal rings and **swings** filled the **spacious** enclosures. In addition to the **wire netting**, the enclosures were protected by large panes of glass that stopped people from feeding the animals.

As sharp-eyed Isy soon realized, it was utterly impossible for anyone to steal so much as a **flea**. In order to run off with a monkey, the thief would have to get inside the heart of the building where he could enter the cages via the inside door. Maybe there was a way of tunnelling up through the floors of the enclosures? In crime movies that was a favourite method for stealing diamonds or robbing a bank. But the monkey population was only small ... Surely someone would notice if a monkey disappeared? Although ...

"That's it!" cried Isy, announcing her theory triumphantly to Amanda. "The zoo keepers must be in it together!" But when she turned to face her friend,

---

to make sth up – etwas erfinden;
stump – Stumpf;
swing – Schaukel;
spacious – geräumig;
wire netting – Maschendraht; flea – Floh

Amanda had **vanished** without a trace. She hurried past the cages in confusion. Nothing. No sign of Amanda.

Instead she saw a group of **silvery gibbons** and an elderly lady with a grey bun and fashionable pink glasses. She looked somehow familiar, and her smile seemed to indicate that she recognized Isy, too. Then it all became clear. It was the nice old lady who'd warned Amanda about leaving her bag unsupervised. Well, she'd certainly been right about that!

"I see you like the zoo then," the old woman said in a bright voice that didn't seem quite **appropriate** for her age.

"It's a school project," explained Isy. "But right now I'm looking for my friend."

"I think she's at the entrance." The old woman nodded at her and continued slowly on her way.

She was right. Isy found Amanda at the entrance to the monkey house. She was chatting to a young man with **striking** red hair, who was leaning **nonchalantly** against a **cart** with the words "Monkey House" written on its side. Isy guessed that he worked there. The first thing she noticed was that Amanda was pretending to be grown-up again. She even had a cigarette in her hand. It was **pathetic**! As soon as she noticed Isy, Amanda came running towards her.

---

to vanish – verschwinden;
silvery gibbon – Silbergibbon;
appropriate – geeignet;
striking – auffallend;
nonchalant – lässig;
cart – Karre;
pathetic – hier: affig

"What do you **reckon**?" she giggled. "His friends call him Carrot!"

She made a big show of taking another puff of her cigarette and added, "By the way, your theory's all nonsense. None of the monkeys have gone missing! The only place you'll find the mafia is in Mr Rimpau's book. So you can forget all about it, OK?"

---

to reckon – glauben

– 6 –

Forget all about it? Not likely! Amanda could say what she liked, but Isy had no **intention** of dropping her theory just because some red-haired guy thought he knew best. She certainly wasn't ready to stop her investigation yet. The events at the zoo were on her mind throughout the entire day, from the moment she turned on the radio at breakfast and sat down to eat her toast and jam, until last thing at night when she brushed her long wavy hair in front of the mirror.

She couldn't help wondering why the Goth hadn't contacted them. Surely there should have been a notice in the paper, offering a holdall of gym kit in exchange for a brown capuchin monkey? After all, the monkey was worth ten thousand Euros!

Isy knew that every investigation included phases of frustration, and she was experiencing one right now. There was something in the air, and her nose was **twitching** in anticipation, but she couldn't start the hunt. There were no real **leads** or clues. Isy was acquainted with this kind of situation from countless books and films. She was **stumbling** blindly in a fog of speculation, but one thing was certain: there was a trail leading back to the zoo. Not a particularly warm trail

---

intention – Absicht;
to twitch – jucken;
lead – Hinweis;
to stumble – stolpern

perhaps, but she couldn't afford to let it go cold. With that thought in mind, she reached decisively for the telephone in order to get Amanda out of bed. It was Saturday morning.

"Isy?" Her friend yawned loudly. "What's up?"

"Let's go to the zoo!"

"Are you crazy? It's the weekend!"

"So what! There's loads to do."

"We've got *ages* before we have to hand in the assignment!"

"Listen, do you want to go to Philadelphia or don't you?"

"What's it got to do with Philadelphia? Why do you have to be so **bossy**?'

"Because I get the feeling that I'm doing all the work round here!"

"And I get the feeling you just want to **snoop around** the zoo!" said Amanda suspiciously. But in the end, she gave in and agreed.

"Isy's suffering from zoo-eritis!" she told her parents as she snatched a roll from the breakfast table and ran out of the door.

They met at the lion gate and spent the whole weekend at the zoo – not to mention almost every afternoon of the following week. They saw **ibexes, seals,** sea lions and penguins, as well as a family of **beavers** asleep within the glass walls of their artificial lodge.

Isy read out the names of the animals and their countries of origin while Amanda entered the details in her

---

bossy – hier: zickig;
to snoop around – herumschnüffeln;
ibex – Steinbock;
seal – Robbe;
beaver – Biber

neatly written notes. There was a file on her computer with the title "Berlin Zoo" and she updated it regularly. Sometimes Isy added a black cross to the name of a particular species to show that it might be at risk from the mafia. Two black crosses meant that the danger was acute. Small rare animals, for example, could easily be stolen from the zoo. But there was no real way of knowing what kind of animals would attract a criminal's interest.

Amanda had seen through her, of course. The web assignment wasn't Isy's only reason for visiting the zoo. She was snooping around like Miss Marple's great-granddaughter.

On one occasion, when they'd sneaked past a no-entry sign into a **maintenance area** to take a look at a loading ramp **piled** high with green **crates**, a man with a brown beard had chased them away.

"What do you think you're doing snooping around here? Didn't you see the sign? Now get away from here and stick to the paths that you're allowed on!"

What was he trying to hide from them? They'd take another look later, Isy decided. This time the crates had been empty. "Live Animals!", it had said on the labels. Well, there was sure to be a time when they'd be able to investigate **undisturbed**. They needed to find out what was usually kept inside those crates. Baby capuchin monkeys perhaps?

With the exception of that incident, they felt quite at home in the zoo. Nature had **woven** an invisible web

---

maintenance area – Wirtschaftshof;
to pile – stapeln;
crate – Kiste;
undisturbed – ungestört;
to weave – weben

around the peaceful green **refuge** at the heart of the city. The zoo was a different world. The grey skyline of offices and the twinkling lights of the neon signs were the only indication that Berlin was close at hand. Here, in this closed world of strange smells and noises, you could imagine you were on a trip around the world. Within the space of a few steps you could see animals from all four corners of the globe.

They even had their personal favourites. Amanda's was a fat **pygmy hippopotamus**, while Isy loved the two **marabou storks** that sat in the **aviary** with their heads tucked into their feathers, occasionally eyeing the visitors with a kindly gaze. Were they really as clever as people said?

During their outings they often **bumped into** the old lady with the pink glasses who was obviously one of the zoo's loyal visitors. She always seemed to be knitting.

On the fourth afternoon they went into the aquarium to ask about Amanda's bag, and when they came out, two of their classmates were standing on the steps. Tannhäuser and Jelly Baby! They would never have expected to see them here.

"Are you seeing what I'm seeing?" said Amanda in surprise. "That's Reginald and Hagen! What are they doing here?"

"No idea!" said Isy. The brain box of 7b on a trip to the zoo with the laziest pupil in the class? Isy hadn't even realized they were friends!

---

refuge – Zuflucht;
pygmy hippopotamus – Zwergflusspferd;
marabou stork – Marabu;
aviary – Voliere;
to bump into sb – jmdn. zufällig treffen

Two days later it all became clear: Tannhäuser and Jelly Baby weren't visiting the zoo for fun. They were studying it.

The next time they saw the boys, Tannhäuser and Jelly Baby were examining the information boards in the bear house.

"Well, what a coincidence!" **trilled** Amanda. "What are *you* doing here?"

"None of your business," said Jelly Baby, chewing noisily on a mouthful of jelly babies.

Tannhäuser gave them a surprised-looking smile. Then he put his hand to his mouth and muttered into a miniature tape recorder, "The black bear, also known as the **cinnamon** bear or *Ursus americanus*, can be found throughout North America, while the brown bear is native to both North America and Eurasia ..."

What were they doing? The zoo wasn't even their territory. Tannhäuser had chosen the opera!

"**Beat it!**" said Isy. "The zoo belongs to us!"

"Why should the zoo belong to you?" Tannhäuser **objected**.

He was smaller than Jelly Baby and quite skinny like most vegetarians. There was a rumour that he secretly drank brandy. He liked to **annoy** people with his clever comments. At the ice-cream van, for example, he'd ask for three scoops of **orchid** ice-cream, so as to be able to tell the baffled ice-cream man that vanilla was an orchid genus from South America. The truth

---

to trill – flöten;
cinnamon – Zimt;
Beat it! – Hau ab!;
to object – widersprechen;
to annoy – ärgern;
orchid – Orchidee

was that Tannhäuser was the Einstein of 7b. Sometimes he even played the cello at school concerts as well.

"Yeah, why should the zoo belong to you?" echoed Jelly Baby.

"Because we were here first, you creep!" hissed Amanda.

Jelly Baby let out a **whinny** of protest, then squinted at them through his bright blue eyes and pretended to shoot Amanda with his hand: "Bang bang!"

That was typical. Once during a history lesson he'd even fired a blank cartridge, right in the middle of the **Peasants' War**.

"Clear off!" said Amanda. "And take your head somewhere else – I'm allergic to **straw**, you know! Besides, you're not on my level."

"Did you hear what she said?" Jelly Baby grunted in the direction of his new-found friend. "I'm not on her level! What's that supposed to mean?"

"What she means," said Tannhäuser, "is that her dad's an accountant, whereas your dad's **on the dole**."

"That's not what I meant at all!" protested Amanda with a **blush**. "It's just that Jelly Baby's always so rude!"

Isy looked coolly at the boys. "Who gave you your special passes then?"

"We don't need special passes. We're doing things differently."

"How?" demanded Amanda. "Don't tell me you descended from the sky!"

---

whinny – Wiehern;
Peasant's War – Bauernkrieg;
straw – Stroh;
to be on the dole – arbeitslos sein;
blush – Erröten

"Wouldn't you like to know?" said Jelly Baby with a grin.

"Listen, why don't you guys do the other zoo instead," suggested Isy.

"If you're so keen on the idea, why don't you?" Tannhäuser slipped the tape recorder inside his jeans pocket.

"Which other zoo?" asked Amanda in surprise.

"Our zoo, in *East* Berlin!" snorted Jelly Baby. "It's twice as big as this one. Surely you must have heard of it? Still an arrogant West German, aren't you, roly-poly?"

"I know more about East Berlin than you do!" **squealed** Amanda.

Isy signalled to her friend. "Come on, let's go. We're wasting our time. Tomorrow morning we can speak to Dr Trisch."

Dr Trisch was in the middle of eating a cheese sandwich when the two girls interrupted his morning break. They described the situation and asked for his help, but their teacher refused. According to him, Reginald and Hagen had every right to focus on whichever part of Berlin they liked. The same thing had happened in other classes, and there was nothing anyone could do. In any case, it made the competition all the more interesting.

"I'm afraid there's only one thing for it!" said Trischi, sweeping the crumbs off his **chequered** jacket. "If you want to **win** the competition, you'll just have

---

to squeal – schreien;
chequered – kariert;
to win – gewinnen, schlagen

to make sure you're the best! Now if you'll excuse me, ladies ..." And with that he hurried over to the other side of the playground to break up a fight.

The girls returned to the classroom in disappointment. They were back where they'd started. So they were supposed to make sure they were the best ... That was easier said than done with Reginald and Hagen behind them like a pair of **evil spirits**. It was bad enough knowing that they'd be forced to see them every minute of the day.

"We'll have to scare them off!" decided Amanda. She wrote a note on a tiny scrap of paper, folded it and passed it forwards to Isy.

Hidden from their teacher by Jelly Baby's broad back, her friend read the message: "Dear Isy, why don't we go around and swap all the labels on the cages? What do you think? Love, Amanda."

Isy wrote her response on the other side: "Dear Amanda, what a fantastic idea! How many centuries have we got? Love, Isy."

All they could think about for the rest of the day was how they could chase the boys away from the zoo. They kept coming up with different plans, but in the end, they reached the same conclusion as their teacher: the only way they could beat Tannhäuser and Jelly Baby was by making sure their project was the best!

"We have to find out more about the zoo!" said Isy. "Information is everything. Being properly informed is half the battle. What do you say we call in on the director tomorrow morning?" They were standing in the well-stocked **aisles** of a supermarket where Isy was

---

evil spirit – böser Geist;
aisle – Gang

ticking off the items from the shopping-list: potato powder, tea, vinegar, **flaked almonds** and cat food.

"But I'm busy tomorrow."

"Too bad! We can't let them catch up with us, Amanda!"

"Mum's already asking why I don't just set up home in the zoo!" She manoeuvred an orange-coloured packet of tea from the shelf and threw it into Isy's trolley. "There you go! One pack of tea!"

"Hey! Hang on a second! You haven't even checked the price!" Isy fished the tea back out. "So are you coming with me or not?"

"OK, but just this once! Promise you won't ask me to go again!"

"I promise," Isy said **solemnly**.

"If you stick to your word, I'll have a surprise for you tomorrow!" announced Amanda. "It begins with a 't'!"

---

flaked almonds – Mandelplättchen;
solemn – feierlich

– 7 –

The surprise was a small black tape recorder, just like the one certain other people were using in the zoo. Amanda handed it to Isy triumphantly as they stood shivering at the train station after school.

It seemed as though winter had returned. Thick white snowflakes whirled gently through the air. It was like being in a giant glass snowglobe that had been shaken by an invisible hand and carefully put back down.

Isy examined the tape recorder **in delight**. "Amanda, you're a star! Where did you get it from?"

"It's my dad's. He uses it at work to dictate letters to his secretary."

"Brilliant! That'll save us **loads of** time!"

Feeling pleased with herself, Isy dropped the tape recorder into her coat pocket. It still felt warm from Amanda's hands. She didn't get it out again until they had arrived at the zoo's main office and were knocking on the director's door.

"Do you have an appointment?" asked his secretary in surprise. Her boss was away from the office on business. Besides, in her opinion, the press officer and not the director was the person to speak to.

"So where can we find the press officer?" Isy asked.

"In Finland," the woman said sweetly.

---

in delight – entzückt;
loads of – massenhaft

In the end, she took pity on them and tried to find them a zoologist to talk to. Things didn't look hopeful. Everyone was out of the office that afternoon. In the end, Mr Knöpfle, a zoologist with a smile like Brad Pitt's, turned up to take them to his office and give them a few minutes of his time. After that he had an urgent meeting in the seabird enclosure.

His office was small and very chilly. In spite of the cold weather the window overlooking the grounds of the zoo was wide open. "It's because of the new **carpet**," Mr Knöpfle informed them when he saw Isy's look. "It absolutely stinks! I'm trying to get some air to it!"

He offered them a seat, then perched on the edge of his desk, next to a collection of framed photographs. Isy looked at the photo of a woman with long blonde hair – probably his girlfriend, she thought. She told him all about the school assignment, not forgetting to mention the winning group's prize.

Mr Knöpfle seemed to understand that their web report had to be better than everyone else's. "Philadelphia is just *wonderful!*" he said enthusiastically.

"Have you been there?" asked Amanda. The zoologist shook his head and pointed to the photo of the blonde woman. "Sadly not. But my sister Marcella works in Stuttgart and often flies there on business."

So the blonde woman wasn't his girlfriend! Isy wondered whether Benedikt would ever put a photo of her on his desk. Ha, not likely! But Mr Knöpfle was more than just a loving brother; he was a really attractive guy.

Isy looked **approvingly** at his jeans, his pullover and

---

carpet – Teppichboden;
approving – beifällig

his shining eyes. They were all the same shade of blue. And his skin was fantastically **tanned**. But the best thing about him was his **cosy**-sounding accent. Every word seemed to plop from his mouth like a soft, round bubble. He was very helpful when she asked him for some printed information.

Opening his desk, he equipped them with a glossy brochure and map that had been published to mark the zoo's 150th anniversary. Then he helpfully disappeared into the press officer's room and returned with an armful of posters and leaflets, which the two girls stowed enthusiastically inside their bags.

Isy had only just started the tape recorder and was about to ask her first question when the zoologist glanced at the time. They took the **hint** and got up from their chairs, but Isy could barely hide her disappointment. There was still so much they wanted to know!

"Could we come back again another time?" she asked. "We'd like to know how a zoo like this works."

Mr Knöpfle had already put on his waterproof jacket. He opened the door. "But of course! Just give me a call! We'll set up a new appointment and maybe even do a tour."

"That would be fab. Do you really mean that?"

"You have my word."

The three of them walked outside together, then the zoologist hurried away with a friendly goodbye, taking long fast **strides** towards the bird house.

---

tanned – gebräunt;
cosy – gemütlich;
hint – Wink;
stride – Schritt

Isy watched him go. “What did he say?” she asked in confusion.

“Oh, he’s from **Swabia**!” the cosmopolitan Amanda informed her. “They always talk like that!” They **leafed through** the anniversary brochure together. “So what now?”

“We haven’t been to see the pandas for a while.”

“Pandas? We haven’t seen a film for even longer! Come on, I’ll **treat** you to a ticket!”

They left the zoo and strolled over to the famous cinema complex at the station. An action film was showing.

“Hey, cool!” Amanda said happily. “A thriller! Actually, any film would be fine, so long as it’s not about animals. I never want to see another animal again! Did I tell you that two large bars of soap have gone missing at home? Guess who ate them?”

“Surely monkeys don’t eat soap!” exclaimed Isy in astonishment, **rummaging** through her pockets in search of some change to buy popcorn. Then she had the shock of her life. Her leather wallet was in there, but where on earth was Amanda’s tape recorder? She could **distinctly** remember turning it on whilst they were in Mr Knöpfle’s office.

“You go ahead, Amanda, I won’t be a moment!” she said in a small voice. “I think I left your tape recorder behind. Leave my ticket at the counter!”

Without stopping to look at Amanda’s horrified expression, she ran off in the direction of the zoo. She

---

Swabia – Schwaben;
to leaf through – durchblättern;
to treat sb – jmdn. einladen;
to rummage – wühlen;
distinct – deutlich

was probably setting a world sprinting record for girls of her age. Gasping for breath, she ran into the building and raced down the corridors past an astonished-looking Carrot, only to find that the secretary had gone. Her office was empty, with her rotating chair pointing towards the door. There was a humming noise, as the fax machine printed a sheet of paper.

Well, she'd just have to try Mr Knöpfle directly. Isy gave a quiet knock at the door, but nothing happened. The Swabian obviously hadn't got back yet. Isy hesitated for a second, then pushed down the handle and walked into the office that they'd left only minutes before.

The window was still wide open. One of the two **shutters** was clattering in the wind. There was quite a breeze. Most important of all though, the tape recorder was lying on the desk. With a **sigh of relief**, she picked it up. Maybe it had recorded something? She pressed the "on" button impatiently, but it seemed to be on already. That was funny. Had she forgotten to switch it off?

She rewound the tape until she suddenly heard the sound of a whispered **male** voice. There was no doubt about it: it was coming from the tape. Before Isy had a chance to work out how it had got there, she suddenly froze. The stranger on the tape was whispering about *them*! There was no other way of interpreting what she was hearing. The man was describing her and her friend! **Paralysed** with horror, she listened to the voice.

---

shutter – Fensterladen;
sigh of relief – Seufzer der Erleichterung;
male – männlich;
paralysed – gelähmt

"A fat one and a skinny one! I'd say they're thirteen or fourteen years old. I noticed them right away because they've been snooping around. But you're never going to believe this: they were chatting about the mafia and contract crime!"

For a moment the tape went silent. All Isy could hear was an **odd** rattling noise. Then the whispering continued. "What do you reckon? Should I take care of them?"

She'd heard enough! Hands shaking, she switched off the recorder and ran from the room. Her heart was beating so fast it felt like it was going to burst. What was going on? Who did the voice belong to? And how had it got there? Why did the mysterious man know all about them?

Isy's mind was racing. It looked as though they were really in danger! It seemed to take forever to run to the cinema.

Sweaty and tired, she collected her ticket from the counter and then dragged Amanda out of her comfortable cinema seat and led her through the dark.

"Hey! What do you think you're doing?" Amanda protested through a mouthful of popcorn. "Sit down and watch the film! It's unbelievably exciting."

"Trust me: it's nothing like as exciting as this!"

---

odd – seltsam

– 8 –

It was so quiet in the classroom that you could hear a pin drop. After some initial restlessness, the pupils of 7b had settled down with their Maths books and were concentrating on their work. They had one period in which to solve a series of difficult Maths problems. A sports lesson was going on outside, and they could hear balls bouncing on the playground. Warm March sunshine came through the windows.

Tannhäuser was the first to finish, followed by Jennifer and then Isy. They handed in their books.

Isy walked past Amanda's desk and saw the look of **despair** on her face. Amanda had been in a bad way since the **previous** day. Now she was even more tired and stressed: firstly because she hadn't been able to sleep that night; and secondly because she was completely hopeless at Maths.

Trying not to ruin the others' concentration, Isy sat down quietly and focused on the mystery of the monkey and the tape. She wrote down the names of everyone connected to the zoo. The list was quite short. They hadn't been investigating for very long yet. No matter how hard she tried to solve the puzzle, none of the information seemed to add up!

At first she suspected that the voice on the tape belonged to the man who had chased them away from

---

despair – Verzweiflung;
previous – vorige/r

the maintenance area and stopped them from examining the mysterious green crates. But that couldn't be right. The man in the maintenance area had spoken with a thick accent. In the end, Isy was left with more questions: Who was mystery man? Why was he watching them? Who had he been talking to? And what was that odd rattling noise on the tape?

Together with Amanda, she'd played the recording over and over again, listening to the stranger's voice. At first Amanda was mainly **annoyed** by the description of her as "fat", but soon she was just as worried as Isy. With a shudder, they realized that they had stumbled upon something very dangerous indeed. It looked as though they had interrupted someone's plans, and their **suspicions** about contract crime had raised the alarm. The strange thing was that neither she nor Amanda had mentioned the mafia to anyone else. Or maybe Amanda had said something after all? As soon as the lesson was over, she'd have to question her friend.

It was just as Isy had suspected. At first Amanda denied everything, although she went very red. She must have remembered the truth, but she refused to tell Isy until they were halfway home. Yes, on one occasion she *had* mentioned the mafia to someone. And it was possible that she'd also said something about contract crime. Who was that someone?

"Carrot," Amanda said **reluctantly**.

"What? You've been talking to Carrot?"

"Only once! It was in the monkey house, remem-

---

to be annoyed – verärgert sein;
suspicion – Verdacht;
reluctant – widerwillig

ber?" Amanda sounded irritated. "You *saw* me talking to him. I just wanted to find out whether any of that stuff you'd been telling me about the mafia was actually true. I asked him if any monkeys were missing."

So it was Carrot! Carrot worked in the monkey house, and what's more, she'd seen him near Mr Knöpfle's office. Yet the voice on the tape didn't belong to him. They would have recognized him straightaway.

"Did you tell him about the monkey?"

"I'm not stupid!" Amanda said angrily. "And anyway, you can't seriously think that Carrot's involved with the mafia!"

"How can we be sure? All I know is that we need to come up with a plan." Isy blew warm air onto her hands and looked around helplessly. "By the way, do you know his real name?"

They were standing in front of the travel agency again. The life-size camel and the plastic palm tree were still there. An Easter trip to Egypt! It would be amazing to lie on the sand, sleeping in the sun …

"Patrick Talke."

"Patrick," Isy echoed. It was the right name for someone with red hair. But she was keen to get home. "Come on, let's go. I'm really hungry!"

"Come back to my place then," suggested Amanda. "I'll cook *spaghetti negri.*"

Spaghetti negri were sticks of pasta that had been coloured black by adding **cuttlefish** ink. Whilst they were still in the packet, they looked like black wire.

Amanda's career as a **chef** had begun last autumn in Altgrünheide with a pack of spaghetti. Since then, she'd turned into a real culinary genius, thanks to

---

cuttlefish – Tintenfisch; chef – Koch/Köchin

financial help from her **grateful** father. Fed up with her mum's constant dieting, Amanda courageously tried her hand at anything, stuffing cannelloni, preparing pizzas, inventing new salads and even experimenting with polenta, which was her dad's favourite food. Not everything that she attempted worked out first time, but Amanda kept trying all the same.

Isy couldn't understand why her friend liked *spaghetti negri*. No **amount** of butter and grated cheese could stop it tasting like wet **cardboard**. But it was full of energy at least.

The two friends were sitting in the shiny white kitchen in Amanda's enormous flat, while Monki, as Amanda had **christened** him, towered above them on top of the fridge, peeling a banana. No one would ever have guessed that he liked eating soap.

"It looks as though he's really made himself at home."

"Don't say that! Our cleaning lady has **threatened** to resign if he stays any longer." Amanda looked at her accusingly and showed her four red dots. "We've all got them. I think Monki's got fleas! Mum wants to know when the sanctuary can take him. You've got to think of something, Isy. What am I going to do when she realizes that I've been lying to her? She'll probably throw me out. Monki and I will have to move in with you. Is that what you want?"

"OK, OK! I've got a plan. It's a pretty mad idea, and it won't work straightaway."

---

grateful – dankbar;
amount – Menge;
cardboard – Pappe;
to christen – taufen;
to threaten – drohen

"I don't care, so long as it works in the end! You've got no idea what I'm going through."

Amanda pulled out a handkerchief and blew her nose. Then she took another generous helping of spaghetti. Once the sticks of pasta had been boiled, they turned the colour of anthracite. She started telling Isy about her latest dream. It was about cooking again.

"This time I was preparing dinner for my parents. Just as I'd finished cooking, a group of Polynesian tourists knocked on the door, saying that I'd invited them for dinner. Of course, we didn't have nearly enough food, but everyone was starving and they all started banging on the table. I can hear the noise now."

"Why didn't you send them to McDonald's?" Isy laughed. "Your dreams are always really weird, you know."

After lunch they went upstairs to Amanda's bedroom and lit some long thin **sticks of incense**. Then Amanda gave her favourite cactus a little drop of water and put on a Kelly Family CD. Isy was just pleased not to have to listen to "Candle in the Wind" again. Amanda usually played it over and over again, becoming sadder and sadder each time.

Isy had settled down on her friend's armchair. It was made of transparent blue plastic and had been blown up like a balloon. The Japanese shop sold them and everyone wanted one. Naturally Amanda, who always had everything, had been given one for Christmas.

The room filled with the exotic smell of incense, and Isy concentrated on finding a way to get the red-haired zoo keeper to talk. She was worried that he wouldn't take them seriously.

---

stick of incense – Räucherstäbchen

"I think you'll have to borrow another cigarette from Carrot," she said, thinking aloud.

"Why me?" exclaimed Amanda in horror.

"Because I don't smoke, do I? Besides, he's bound to think you're older."

Isy had to be careful not to laugh, but the compliment worked. Amanda agreed to cooperate, so Isy described the rest of the plan.

"We have to find out whether he's part of the mafia or whether he just told someone what we said. He might be friends with those Goths, for example. We need to phone him, so you can tell him that you're in a difficult position because something you told him has become public news. You feel as though you're being watched, and you need him to tell you what happened. Appeal to his sense of honour!"

"Do you think it will work?"

"What, if you flirt with him like before?"

"Te-he-he," laughed Amanda. "Red-heads aren't my type!" All the same, she agreed to ask Carrot to meet up with her. Isy phoned the zoo. She gave the receiver to Amanda.

"Who should I say I am?" her friend stuttered.

"Just say you're his mum!"

It took a while for anyone to answer and even longer to be connected to the person they needed.

"Hello, Carrot!" chuckled Amanda. "It's your mum!"

– 9 –

Two days later it was time for their appointment with Carrot. After some **hesitation** he had promised to meet Amanda outside the crocodile enclosure in the aquarium.

Instead of heading straight for the zoo, they stopped off at the travel agency. When they left the shop again, there was a fantastic new attraction in its window. Right next to the life-size camel a monkey was swinging on the plastic palm. The owner of the travel agency had welcomed Monki with open arms. She'd studied zoology and worked for a few years at her father's veterinary practice before marrying a travel agent. Monki would be in safe hands until the window display was changed after Easter. With a sigh of relief, the two girls continued on their way.

"Sorry, still no sign of your bag!" the **porter** called out as they rushed up the steps to the aquarium. They still had **plenty of** time to spare when they reached the wooden bridge that led towards the glass-walled crocodile enclosure. Its jungle-green interior was in the middle of the aquarium's first floor. A wave of warm, fishy air swept towards them, making it almost impossible to breathe. Carrot wasn't there yet. The bridge was empty.

---

hesitation – Zögern;
porter – Pförtner;
plenty of – jede Menge

They glanced around uncertainly. **Beneath** them was an artificial river lined with tropical plants. Enormous crocodiles were lying on the stony bottom like grey **concrete** sculptures.

"Remember that bit in *Jurassic Park*?" Amanda said in a high voice. She was holding her nose. "You know, when the dinosaurs attack the café and chase the kids into the kitchen."

Isy looked down nervously. Crocodiles weren't the same as dinosaurs, of course, but *Jurassic Park* was fiction. These creatures were real!

At first it looked as though they were paralysed or very sleepy, but Isy knew better: the crocodiles were waiting for some food to appear – something tasty, like Isy or Amanda, **for instance**. Of all the places that the zoo keeper could have suggested, this had to be the least romantic. Maybe he had other reasons for meeting them there …

For a moment Isy wondered whether it was safe to leave her friend alone, then she pulled herself together and whispered in Amanda's ear, "I'm off now! Don't worry: I'll be watching you."

"Why should I be worried?" **squawked** Amanda. It was lucky she had such an underdeveloped imagination!

Isy quickly left the bridge in order to hide herself in the leaves of an enormous **rubber tree** just outside the crocodile enclosure. She had a good view of Amanda and would easily be able to see if Carrot was alone. It

---

beneath – unter;
concrete – Beton;
for instance – zum Beispiel;
to squawk – hier: protestieren;
rubber tree – Gummibaum

took a long time for anything to happen, but at last a mop of bright red hair appeared at the other end of the hall. Carrot! She could barely recognize him without his uniform. Instead of his usual overalls he was dressed in black leather, which made him look really cool. As soon as she saw him, Isy was struck by a sudden idea. She would have to tell Amanda! First of all though, she kept watching Patrick Talke. He seemed nervous! He kept glancing around him – perhaps he was being followed?

Before Isy had a chance to see if anyone was behind him, the zoo keeper marched towards the exit. He was heading towards her! Isy hid among the leaves. She didn't want Carrot to **tread on** her toes. Why was he leaving already? Amanda seemed cross when Isy appeared beside her on the bridge.

"What's wrong with him?" she moaned. "First it's the crocodile enclosure, and now it's the **nocturnal house**. I'm supposed to be there in ten minutes."

The nocturnal house was located in the basement of the bird house. They'd been meaning to go there for ages. Carrot must have decided to trick whoever was following him with a last-minute change of place.

Full of nervous excitement, Isy left the aquarium, followed by a **bad-tempered** Amanda. On their way to the new meeting place they walked past a group of gardeners who were planting denim-blue **pansies** and yellow primroses in the **crusty soil**. The zoo seemed to be

---

to tread on – treten auf;
nocturnal house – Nachttierhaus;
bad-tempered – schlecht gelaunt;
pansy – Stiefmütterchen;
crusty – verkrustet;
soil – Boden

preparing itself slowly for the traditional Easter rush of visitors. The smell of fresh earth reminded Isy of Granny Dora's garden. Ever since she could remember, she'd had her own flowerbed there. Each year, as soon as spring was approaching, she'd plant packs of mysterious seeds and wait impatiently to see the results of her gardening.

"Did you hear what the porter said earlier?" Amanda said suddenly. "There's still no sign of my bag. I absolutely knew it! That's the last we'll ever hear of that Goth."

"You need to be more patient!"

"It's all very well for you to say that. We should have sold the monkey to the travel agency right away!"

"We were lucky that the travel agency agreed to take care of him. You know that, Amanda! What's wrong with you? Have you been having trouble with your parents again?"

"My parents? No, they haven't said a word. They seem to have forgotten how to talk!"

It wasn't the first time that Amanda had announced that her parents weren't speaking to each other. Isy thought it must be awful for her. Isy's parents sometimes shouted at each other, but it never lasted for long.

"Well, I hope *you* haven't forgotten how to talk, Amanda! Everything depends on you getting him to tell you everything." They had arrived at the bird house and were making their way downstairs.

Amanda was about to say something when it suddenly went dark. What was going on? A **power cut**? Amanda **stopped short**.

---

power cut – Stromausfall;
to stop short – hier: stehen bleiben

"Are you sure you want to carry on?" she whispered unhappily.

"He's waiting for you, remember!"

Isy felt her way forwards until she could see the silhouettes of other people. Oddly enough, no one seemed to mind the darkness. The visitors made their way carefully through the room. Isy held Amanda's hand in a **tight** grip.

Gradually, their eyes adapted to the dark. Now they could see that the walls were made of panes of glass, behind which animals were going about their lives under the light of an artificial moon. Thanks to electric lighting, daytime could be turned into night and night into day. Suddenly it all made sense to Isy. Nocturnal animals were only active in the dark, so by turning the lights off, the zoo made it possible for visitors to see the creatures moving and eating. But how were they supposed to find Carrot in the dark?

Amanda seemed to be thinking the same thing. "Does he expect me to play **Blind Man's Buff** with him or something?" she whispered in **annoyance**.

"Come on, Amanda," Isy **begged** her. "Surely you want to find out who's been spying on us?"

"But this place is so scary!"

"Carrot must feel safer here than with the crocodiles," Isy said in a low voice. "I didn't really want to tell you, but I think he's being followed. I'm sure he'll be waiting for you somewhere. Go on, take a look for him."

---

tight – fest;
Blind Man's Buff – blinde Kuh;
annoyance – Verärgerung;
to beg – bitten

"What about you?"

"I'll wait here. Just shout if anything happens."

There was a moment's silence. Isy could hear Amanda breathing. Then she vanished into the darkness.

Isy glanced around in relief. She was standing in front of an enormous pane of glass looking into a terrarium. According to the description, it was home to a family of **aardvarks** or "earth pigs" as they were originally called. With their long legs, **floppy ears** and big noses, they looked like cartoon characters. Isy was reminded of a song by the Prinzen: *In this world of ours you've got to be a swine…* She used to sing it with Amanda all the time.

Hopefully Amanda would get some information from Carrot. She didn't know why, but she was starting to feel worried. Something wasn't quite right. She could practically see there was trouble. Was Amanda's nervousness starting to get the better of her, too?

She turned decisively towards the aardvarks' neighbour, an Australian **mole**.

Suddenly someone screamed. She'd known it! It had to be Amanda. Without stopping to think, Isy ran in the direction of the noise, crashing into people and banging her knees, until Amanda fell into her arms.

"What happened?" Isy gasped. "Where's Carrot?"

"I don't know," stammered Amanda, "but there's a body in the corner. I nearly tripped over it."

"What?" Isy felt herself go weak at the knees, but she walked forwards and almost screamed with shock:

---

aardvark – Erdferkel;
floppy ears – Schlappohren;
mole – Maulwurf

in front of one of the enclosures a body was lying on the ground.

"Help!" she cried weakly. "Help! There's someone on the floor!"

In no time the darkness came to life. Isy had barely been able to see the other people, but now they rushed towards her, shouting excitedly. One man called for first-aid, whilst a woman announced in a trembling voice that she was just about to collapse.

Isy was the first to bend down towards the body. She could only see its outline, but her fingertips touched smooth, cool leather. Then she was pushed to one side as some of the silhouettes picked up the lifeless body and carried it out of the room. Isy and Amanda hurried after them in silence, running up the stairs. **Blinking** because of the light, they looked nervously at the body. It was Carrot!

Some of the visitors and staff were taking care of the unconscious man. Isy recognized the director's secretary and the old woman with the grey bun. As always when there was an accident, a crowd of onlookers had gathered. To their annoyance, they spotted Tannhäuser's **faded** woolly hat and Jelly Baby's blue-and-white baseball cap. Would they never get rid of those boys?

White-lipped, Amanda grabbed hold of her. "Is he dead?" she asked in a small voice.

"Nonsense! He's just been hit on the head." Isy was trying to sound **reassuring**, but her heart was beating wildly. Hadn't she said from the start that there were

---

to blink – blinzeln;
faded – hier: verwaschen;
reassuring – beruhigend

criminals involved in this business? Amanda would have to believe her now!

Whilst Carrot's rescuers made way for the professional first-aid team, Isy pulled her friend to one side. "Haven't you noticed anything about his clothes?" she whispered. Amanda looked at them. "They're cool! Really cool!" she said.

"Really black, you mean," hissed Isy. "Carrot's a Goth! Now what do you have to say for yourself?" She handed Amanda a newspaper article. "He was holding this when we found him. Thank goodness I got to him first."

"What is it?"

"It seems to be a note for you," said Isy. "It's a recipe: *Robber-style Risotto*. Does that mean anything to you?"

– 10 –

The recipe didn't make sense to Amanda at all. She swore blind that she'd never said anything to Carrot about recipes. Of course, she knew risotto was an Italian dish made with rice, but she didn't have a clue why Carrot had been holding the recipe. The back of the recipe wasn't any help to them either. It was a picture of a nest full of eggs, a motif that appeared in almost every magazine at Easter-time. It couldn't be relevant. "Maybe risotto is a reference to the mafia," said Isy. "It has to mean something!"

But the only person who knew what it meant was Carrot, and he had disappeared. **Apparently**, he hadn't taken long to recover from the incident in the nocturnal house. In fact, as soon as he was better, he'd flown to the **Maldives** with his girlfriend. That had to be a trick, of course. Patrick Talke, otherwise known as Carrot, had vanished, leaving Isy and Amanda to face the mafia on their own.

At least that was the situation when Amanda treated Isy to a pistachio ice-cream at *Georgio's*, her favourite Italian café. Isy liked the café, too. Everything had a mysterious shimmer to it, like the inside of a **mussel**. The delicate curtains shimmered – as did the candlesticks, the carafes and glasses on the white tablecloths, and even Signore Georgio himself, whose dark eyes

---

apparently – scheinbar; Maldives – Malediven;
mussel – Muschel

continually kept watch over his customers to make sure they were happy. But today was different. The two friends ate their ice-cream in silence.

Amanda was the first to say anything. "Do you think he sleeps in a coffin, too?"

"Who, Carrot?" asked Isy. She didn't really have to ask. Amanda could talk of nothing else. "Of course not! Not all Goths sleep in coffins." Then she fell silent again.

"They'll kill us, too, you know," Amanda prophesied darkly. "We should order another serving of ice-cream."

"We should think about who can help us to get out of this mess!"

"The police, maybe."

"Not the police," said Isy. "They'd die of laughter. We've got nothing to tell them apart from speculation."

"We've got the recording! We recorded a voice!"

"We can't even tell them how the voice got on the tape. They'd think we were nuts."

Isy scraped the last green **trickle** of ice-cream from the glass. "We need to find someone we can trust."

"In that case, there's only one person I can think of."

"Same here," said Isy. "Have you got a phonecard?"

They didn't find Mr Rimpau at home. His answerphone redirected them to a place where they would never have expected to find him: in hospital!

The hospital was in the centre of Berlin. Once they'd found it and had been directed to the right **ward**, they only had to get past the bossy blonde sister with the

---

trickle – Rinnsal;
ward – Station

deep voice. At last they found themselves at the author's bedside, unsure of what to do next.

The room smelt like a pharmacy. Warm afternoon sunshine shone through the thin hospital curtains and covered Mr Rimpau's bed in light. There was a bottle of multivitamin juice on his bedside table, together with a glass, an azalea in full bloom and a photo of a dark-haired woman in a ski suit. The author looked pale. He sat up in bed when he saw them.

"You two?" he said in confusion. "Something must be badly wrong!"

"It's about the zoo again!" Isy burst out impatiently. "The Goth won't **get in touch**, and all kinds of weird things keep happening."

"I hope my latest novel hasn't been giving you any funny ideas," said Mr Rimpau suspiciously, pointing to two chairs that were lined up near a table. "I don't want to keep reminding you of the past, but sometimes you do have rather hyperactive imaginations."

"I don't!" objected Amanda, who often claimed she had absolutely no imagination at all. "Isy's the one with a hyperactive imagination. Anyone could tell you that!"

They pulled their chairs closer to his bed and told him their story. They'd remembered to bring the tape recording of the whispered voice which they played several times at Mr Rimpau's **request**. When they finished their account of how Carrot had been attacked in the nocturnal house, the author lay silently in bed. Isy was beginning to think that he'd fallen asleep, but then his eyes opened suddenly.

---

to get in touch – sich melden;
request – Bitte

"Which floor is Mr Knöpfle's office on?"

"The ground floor."

"And what about the window? Did he have the window open?"

"No," claimed Amanda. "It was shut."

"Don't be ridiculous!" said Isy **in disbelief**. "It was wide open! It was freezing in there. Mr Knöpfle said the window had to be open because of the smell from the carpet."

"Was it still open when you went back?"

Isy nodded. She could picture it clearly.

"Everyone makes mistakes, Isy," Amanda said triumphantly. "And this time you're wrong. Mr Knöpfle definitely shut the window – I can see him doing it!"

"That's crazy, Amanda! It was open! The shutters were really noisy, remember? It seemed to be very windy out there." Isy brushed her hair out of her eyes. "Besides, you weren't even there the second time!"

"And where was the tape recorder?" asked Mr Rimpau, ignoring the argument.

"On the desk."

"And I suppose the desk was right beside the open window?"

"Exactly!" said Isy in surprise. Suddenly she realized how the voice had come to be on the tape. "The man must have been talking on a mobile next to the open window, right?"

"Yes. He probably watched you leave with the zoologist. In any case, he only had to glance through the window to see no one was there. He must have thought it was safe to make his report. How was he to know

---

in disbelief – ungläubig

that he was being recorded by an **abandoned** tape recorder? That explains the banging noise, too."

"Wow!" gasped Amanda. "You don't happen to know who hit Carrot, do you?"

Mr Rimpau shook his head. He was starting to look very tired.

"What about robber-style risotto? Does that mean anything to you?"

"Sounds delicious," sighed Mr Rimpau. "Much better than the food I get here."

"We've tired you out," said Isy in concern. "I've only got one more question for you: do you think we should explore the maintenance area? There were lots of green crates on a loading ramp. A man chased us away when we tried to get a look. He seemed pretty angry. He must have had something to hide."

Isy felt a **twitching** in her nose and reached for her handkerchief just in time. "Of course, we would have to go in the evening when no one else is there."

"You'll do no such thing!" The author sounded alarmed. "If you want my advice, you should keep away from the zoo for a while. None of it really makes sense to me, and I think it's just a harmless coincidence. But the mafia don't play games, you know."

"How about you? Did you get into trouble when you were researching *One Murder Too Many at the Zoo*?"

"Oh no, my old friend F.B. was there to look after me. He's a leading expert on the mafia. And of course, some of the story was fiction." Mr Rimpau reached for the glass on his bedside table and drank a little.

---

to abandon – verlassen, zurücklassen;
twitching – Kribbeln

"I think it's amazing the way you get all your ideas," said Isy admiringly.

"Oh, you know what they say: the best ideas are out there – you only have to open your eyes." Mr Rimpau sat up in bed again. "OK, so don't take any unnecessary risks, my dears. I want you to promise that you'll stay away from the zoo until I'm back in action, all right?"

"And when will you be back in action?"

"In about three weeks. I've only just had my **gall bladder** out."

"But we can't wait that long!" said Isy in concern. "Tannhäuser and Jelly Baby will win!"

"So do you promise that you'll stay away from the zoo then?" the author asked them again.

"I promise," said Amanda with a sideways look at Isy, "but you know Isolde! She's already packed her bags for Philadelphia."

Isy had **a face like thunder**, but she shook Mr Rimpau's hand and gave her word. She was still in a bad mood when they left the hospital. She wished she hadn't been forced to make that promise. They'd gone to Mr Rimpau for advice, not to be banned from going to the zoo. If they stuck to their promise, they could forget about winning first prize. It was bye-bye America. They reached the bus stop. Amanda sat down between two women on the graffiti-covered bench and started filing her nails.

"I know you're angry," she said to Isy, who was studying the timetable with a bad-tempered **pout**.

---

gall bladder – Gallenblase;
a face like thunder – ein Gesicht wie zehn Tage Regenwetter;
pout – Schmollmund

"Maybe we should do our report on the Fairy Tale Fountain instead. I'm sure Sassi and Bini wouldn't mind. At least there won't be any gangsters there."

"What about your beloved castle?" Isy said **mockingly**. "Look, that's our bus!"

An enormous yellow bus was heading towards them slowly through the traffic. Of course, there wouldn't be any gangsters at the Fairy Tale Fountain, but did Amanda really think they could **conquer** America with a story about **Little Red Riding Hood** and a statue of a wolf?

"No doubt Tannhäuser and Jelly Baby will be jumping for joy as soon as they hear that we've abandoned the zoo," she said angrily as Amanda got up from the bench unhurriedly. The bus stopped at the edge of the pavement and the doors opened with a hiss.

"You can tell them now, if you like!" exclaimed Amanda, pointing to a blue-and-white baseball cap and a faded woolly hat, whose owners had just left the bus and were disappearing across the street. Surely it couldn't be ... Was she seeing things or was that Reginald and Hagen? Isy stared at them in disbelief. Where were they going? She had to find out. Grabbing hold of her friend, she dragged her across the street.

"Hey! What about our bus?"

"We'll get the next one!"

Filled with excitement and determination, Isy set off after her classmates. Her detective instinct had been **triggered**. After walking down a few streets lined with

---

mocking – spöttisch;
to conquer – erobern;
Little Red Riding Hood – Rotkäppchen;
to trigger – hier: wecken

apartment blocks, shops and cafés, Jelly Baby and Tannhäuser followed a path that bordered the park-like grounds of the zoo. They crossed a bridge and walked along a sandy path next to the canal. The water encircled the zoo like a shimmering liquid **ribbon**. The air smelt of wet leaves, and for the first time that year Isy heard a **blackbird** singing.

"Do we have to go on?" gasped Amanda. "We're in the middle of nowhere."

"I've got a funny feeling about all this," whispered Isy, pulling her friend behind a bush. She'd acted just in time. The very next moment Tannhäuser and Jelly Baby turned round to check that there was no one there. Everything happened unbelievably quickly. The boys climbed up a black metal fence and disappeared from view. So that was how they did it!

"Quick, let's follow them!" Isy ordered, pushing a reluctant and uncooperative Amanda over the fence. Then she pulled herself up and **leaped** down gracefully.

"Are you going to tell me where we are?" snorted Amanda, but Isy just grabbed her hand and pulled her through the bushes onto a path that was filled with other people. They stopped next to an aviary. According to the sign, the creatures on the bare branches were **cattle egrets**.

"Do you recognize it now?"

Even Amanda could see where they were. There was no doubt about it: this was the zoo.

---

ribbon – Band;
blackbird – Amsel;
to leap – springen;
cattle egret – Kuhreiher

"But now we've broken our promise already!" she protested.

"So what? How were we to know that we'd end up in the zoo?" Isy sounded defiant. "Besides, do you see now why Tannhäuser and Jelly Baby don't need special passes for the zoo? They've got their very own entrance. But not for much longer! What do you reckon? Do you think they'll be banned from the zoo when we tell the lady at the gate?"

"Isn't that a bit **mean**?"

"Of course, it's mean, but how else are we supposed to get rid of them?" said Isy crossly. Then she glanced around in satisfaction. "Take a good look at this place, Amanda. This is where we'll be breaking in tomorrow night!"

---

mean – gemein

– 11 –

Sometimes Isy really needed to be alone.

She had followed Benedikt's example and hung a sign on her door with the words "Caution! Land Mines!" Now she was lying on her bed with a new detective novel while Selma purred happily at her feet. But no matter how hard she tried, she couldn't help thinking about the evening ahead of her.

In the end, she gave up on her book and moved to her desk.

Her atlas lay in front of her.

Time and time again she had traced the route across the blue Atlantic, over the green and brown continent, until she reached the little red dot that was Philadelphia. How many of her classmates had been doing the same?

No, she had no intention of allowing her American adventure to be taken away from her just because of a stupid promise she'd made. Nothing and no one was going to come between her and Philadelphia. The trouble was, even Amanda was causing her problems.

That morning her friend hadn't walked to school with her, and she hadn't turned up to lessons either. Later on Mrs Bornstein had phoned to say that her daughter was ill in bed. No one was allowed to visit Amanda until they knew whether her illness was **infectious**. Was nervousness infectious?

---

infectious – ansteckend

Isy was convinced that Amanda wasn't really ill. The previous day they'd come up with a plan that would allow them to break into the maintenance area after dark by climbing over the metal fence into the zoo. They'd be able to snoop around as much as they liked. But now Amanda wouldn't even answer the phone.

Well, Isy was prepared to visit the zoo on her own if she had to. If only she could find another torch! A torch would be **essential** for the adventure. Just as she was getting up from her desk to check her cupboard again, the doorbell rang. Wow! It was bound to be Amanda! Isy wouldn't mind if her friend had **measles**, mumps or the flu. For all she cared, Amanda could be completely yellow with **jaundice** or covered from head to toe in a white **plaster cast** – just so long as she was there!

"I knew you wouldn't let me down!" Isy announced in relief as she threw open the door. But it wasn't Amanda. It was her mother, who was laden with boxes.

Despite her disappointment Isy helped her carry everything into the kitchen.

"What's all this then?"

"It's my new job!" Isy hadn't seen her mum smile like that for a long time. She seemed to have a new hairstyle, too. Her curls bounced up and down as she hurried around the kitchen table, unpacking all the boxes. Inside them were plastic containers of all shapes, sizes and colours.

"It's an established **brand**, you know," her mum

---

essential – wesentlich;
measles – Masern;
jaundice – Gelbsucht;
plaster cast – Gips;
brand – Marke

assured her. "You can make good money with them. And the best part is that I won't be working with computers; I'll be working with people!" Her voice sounded triumphant. "How about you then? Why aren't you at the zoo?"

She was too busy unpacking a cheese container – or a "cheese castle", as it was called – to notice that her daughter hadn't answered. Next came a "salad pavilion", then a "**cucumber** elevator". "What do you make of the names?" she asked uncertainly.

Isy shrugged. For all she cared, the next container could be called "Snow White's **Cauliflower** Coffin'. She would have been happier if her mother had **summoned up her courage** and decided to use a computer.

A few hours later she was on the train, travelling through the glittering evening cityscape. She was excited, but she couldn't help feeling nervous, too. Maybe it wasn't such a good idea to walk around the zoo on her own after dark. But what choice did she have? She couldn't **give in**! She wasn't like Amanda …

Isy **delayed** her decision from station to station until the train arrived at the zoo. Well, now she was there.

Promising herself that she would go home at the first sign of trouble, she set off towards the zoo. In her pocket was the pen torch that she had borrowed from Benedikt. She didn't need it yet. The houses, department stores and theatres of Berlin were shining as bright as a neon sun, and there were plenty of shop-

---

cucumber – Gurke;
cauliflower – Blumenkohl;
to summon up one's courage – seinen Mut zusammennehmen;
to give in – aufgeben;
to delay – verschieben

pers, cinema-goers and other pedestrians on the busy streets.

It was only when she turned into a side road that the lights began to fade. Walking faster, Isy kept glancing around her. Nervously she **buried** her head in her scarf to hide her face.

As she approached the canal, she realized that her heart was beating wildly. This was the darkest part of the route. She could hardly see, but she was going to have to find the fence. Isy was just feeling for Benedikt's torch when another light lit up twenty metres ahead of her. Who could it be? A night watchman working for the zoo? A policeman?

She ducked into the bushes, but the ray of light wandered mercilessly towards her. A figure was approaching from the banks of the canal. Isy saw a head of blonde hair and a black-and-white checked scarf that seemed very familiar …

"Amanda!" she called out in relief. "What are you doing here?"

"Same as you!" said Amanda, gasping for breath. "Gosh, you scared me."

"Well, you scared me!" Isy could hardly believe it. Amanda had come after all! She seemed to have sprung out of nowhere.

"What did you tell your parents?"

"That I'd be sleeping at your place. How about you?"

"**Snap**! But I thought you were supposed to be ill?"

"I was, but now I'm feeling much better. Besides, I had something that belonged to you." She handed Isy

---

to bury – hier: verbergen;
Snap! – das Gleiche!

the torch. Although she hadn't said so, Amanda was trying to tell Isy that she hadn't had the heart to leave her on her own.

"OK, let's go," Isy whispered happily. "We've got to find the fence."

She searched the area with the **beam** from Benedikt's torch. At last the light reached the fence. Once they'd climbed over it, Isy stopped to talk to Amanda for a moment.

"There's nothing to worry about, you know. Nothing can happen to us. There's no one here!"

"But what if the night watchmen find us?"

"We'll hide in the bushes."

They shone their torches on the ground and felt their way forwards until they reached an illuminated path.

"Turn right," Isy whispered loudly. "Towards the bird house!"

The abandoned zoo was sleeping peacefully. The moonlit March night cast shadows over the enclosures and cages. Most of the animals had gone inside, but every now and then they heard a surprised **grunt** or snort.

The zoo seemed to have undergone a mysterious transformation. It looked different in the dark. With every step they took, the bushes and trees became more monstrous, and the illuminated skyline of the city seemed incredibly close.

Isy made the unwelcome discovery that it was harder to **find her bearings** in the dark. Somehow

---

beam – Strahl;
grunt – Grunzen;
to find one's bearings – hier: sich orientieren

they'd managed to go too far to the right, and they found themselves in the adventure playground instead.

"We'll have to cross over to the bear house, Amanda!" she said softly. Suddenly there was a sound of cracking **twigs** coming from somewhere nearby. A bird squawked in protest. For a moment they stood frozen to the spot, listening for noises. Then Amanda threw herself into the bushes with a squeal. Was she crazy? She'd given away their position. Isy crept after her friend and knelt down next to her on the cold earth.

"Let's get out of here!" Amanda said unhappily.

"Shush," hissed Isy.

"But there's someone walking around out there. I heard footsteps!"

"Shush," hissed Isy again, but it was too late.

Two strong arms grabbed her and lifted her into the air. Her eyes and mouth were covered by a piece of soft material that felt like a scarf. Then someone tied her hands behind her back. She kicked out desperately, but her attacker hit her on the back to tell her to start moving. As she stumbled forwards, she thought of Amanda. Had her friend been taken prisoner, too? Maybe she'd managed to escape ...

Isy could sense that she was being led into a room. Her attacker pushed her, and she landed on a soft heap of something – **hay** or straw perhaps. A sack fell to the ground beside her. She held her breath and listened as the footsteps faded into the distance.

Suddenly she realized that she was shaking all over. Her heart was beating so quickly that it was in danger of exploding. Where had they taken her? An unpleas-

---

twig – Zweig;
hay – Heu

ant smell penetrated the material around her eyes and mouth and reached her nose. Had she been **trapped** inside a cage? Surely she wasn't locked up with a troop of wild animals? Sweat ran down her back. What did lions smell like? Or elephants for that matter? Was she imagining things, or was that an animal sniffing around her?

She panicked at the thought of lying next to a huge pair of **jaws**, an elephant's **trunk** or a rhino's horn, and tried to sit up. She needed to shout for help. But how could she shout when her mouth was covered?

Keep calm, Isy told herself. She tried to move on her knees over the straw, but she hit a wooden fence. Maybe that was the answer! She immediately started to rub her head and her nose against the rough wood until the material fell away from her eyes. Soon her mouth was free, too. Her heart sank as she realized that she was surrounded by darkness. And she seemed to have company, too. There was a loud sneeze from the straw beside her.

"Amanda?" she whispered in surprise. "Is that you?"

The straw grunted happily. Amanda had obviously been tied up, too. Surely Amanda wasn't in the sack? Not Amanda with her straw allergy? How wonderful to be together again! Together they were stronger!

"Listen! We're in some kind of enclosure. I'm going to call for help!"

The straw protested wildly.

"What's the matter? Do you want to be trapped in

---

to be trapped – gefangen sein;
jaw – Kiefer;
trunk – Rüssel

here until morning?" said Isy in alarm. "Don't you get it: we could be eaten alive!" She raised her head decisively and shouted for help. Nothing happened, so she waited and then shouted as loudly as she could. Finally, someone seemed to realize they were there. Isy heard footsteps and the sound of voices talking on the other side of the fence.

Suddenly the door opened with a creak and someone asked in a small voice, "Is anyone there?" Then everything happened very quickly.

A pair of torches shone towards them, and the two girls were pulled out of the straw and set free. Isy realized that she'd been **gagged** with her own scarf. Blinking in the light, they stared at their rescuers ...

"Unbelievable!" said Jelly Baby, chewing on his jelly babies. "The calamity queens! Don't tell me that the rest of the class is hidden in here, too!"

At least Tannhäuser seemed worried about them. "Do you know who attacked you?" he said sympathetically.

"No!" lied Isy. She gave Amanda a warning push. Now the panic was over, Amanda started crying with shock, "The mafia attacked us! They've been after us for ages! Isy doesn't want anyone to know."

"The mafia?" **chorused** Tannhäuser and Jelly Baby. "Wow! You'd better tell us everything!"

"Not now!" Isy sounded cross. Why couldn't Amanda keep her mouth shut for a change? "Maybe you should tell *us* what *you're* doing here?"

Tannhäuser held up his tape recorder for the two girls to see. He switched it on, and for a moment it was

---

to be gagged – geknebelt sein;
to chorus – im Chor sagen

silent, then they heard noises from the nocturnal zoo. Horses snorted sleepily, a creature scratched at a fence, an animal grunted in its sleep, and a bird squawked in protest. Finally, Isy heard her own voice screaming for help.

"You see," he said. "We just wanted to record some of the night-time noises in the zoo."

Jelly Baby took over, "Some pig told the zoo that we were climbing over the fence, so now we can only get in at night."

Isy and Amanda looked at each other in embarrassment. Now that was really awkward...

Suddenly there was a sound of movement in the straw, and Amanda rushed nervously towards the door.

"Let's get out of here! The wild animals might attack!"

"Wild animals?" Jelly Baby's face filled with schadenfreude. "You're in a **goat pen**, you idiots!"

---

goat pen – Ziegenstall

– 12 –

The essay topic that morning was: "My Best Friend". In their previous German lesson, they'd talked about "friendship". Now Trischi wanted them to write about it from a personal perspective. Isy, of course, was planning to write about Amanda, but somehow she felt really tired. In the classroom above them some kids were learning a folk song. The constant repetition of the music made Isy feel sleepy. She couldn't wait for the school day to end, but their final period was due to take place with Mrs Müller-Märzdorf. They were visiting a museum. It was the last thing that Isy felt like right now. She cast a sideways look at Amanda, who was yawning like a hippopotamus. After the events of the night before her friend was exhausted as well.

It was amazing that Amanda hadn't flipped out completely. Isy suspected that it was because of the boys. Amanda hadn't wanted to admit that she was frightened.

Some of 7b's pupils put up their hands to ask whether boys could write about girls and girls about boys. Others wanted to know what they should do if they didn't have any friends.

Vanessa called out from the back of the room to ask whether she could write about her dog. Trischi gave a classic teacher's reply. He said he didn't know whether she *could* write about her dog, but she was certainly welcome to try. At long last everyone was staring at their exercise books and scribbling away.

Isy had just started an elegant description of her first

meeting with the newcomer from Nuremberg when she heard a faint **snoring** noise. She glanced at Amanda in horror. But Amanda was busy writing. The noise was coming from in front of her. Dr Trisch had heard it, too. He looked up and stared at Jelly Baby. Isy **prodded** his blue-and-white sweater. It was too late. Over the last few days Hagen Golz had caused nothing but trouble, and now the teacher's anger exploded at the sleeping pupil. He woke with a jump.

Oh no, thought Isy, what if Jelly Baby tells Trischi about last night? She decided to defend her classmate and quickly raised her hand.

"It's not his fault, Dr Trisch! He can't help falling asleep, sir, but I can't tell you why."

"Well, I'm afraid you're going to have to!" Trischi **frowned** at her as severely as he could.

"Don't stop writing," he said to the pupils who had looked up from their work. "You haven't got much time, you know!" He turned to Isy. "As for you, Miss Schütze, we'll talk about this later."

By break-time Trischi seemed to have forgotten that he'd asked Isy to see him. When she stuck her head around the door of the staff room, he was reading the newspaper with a cup of coffee in his hand. He looked up in confusion, then hurriedly finished his coffee and followed her into the corridor, where he stood behind the plant pots on the third floor, peering through the leaves at the schoolkids on the playground below. It was obvious that he expected an explanation. What could she say?

---

to snore – schnarchen;
to prod – schubsen;
to frown – die Stirn runzeln

She couldn't tell him that she and Amanda had slept on an old **dusty** sofa in the basement of Jelly Baby's apartment block. And she certainly couldn't explain that Amanda's idiotic reference to the mafia had resulted in them staying awake until the early hours of the morning. The boys had wanted to know everything about the mysterious events in the zoo, so they'd sat in the cellar talking and eating sandwiches.

But if she told him that, she would have to admit that she and Amanda had entered the zoo after dark and been tied up by nameless, faceless attackers – criminals who wouldn't hesitate to do much worse than lock them in a pen with some harmless Argentinean goats. No, it was out of the question! Dr Trisch would be horrified, and he would force her to promise not to go to the zoo. Isy had no intention of making another promise of that kind.

"I can't say anything more about Jelly Baby," she said **hesitantly**, "because it wouldn't be fair."

"Well, do you call this fair? You've stopped me drinking my coffee!" Her teacher looked disappointed in her. "But thank you anyway."

His politeness made her feel terrible. Isy **blushed**. "OK, then! Amanda and I got into trouble last night, and Hagen and Reginald came to our rescue. They didn't get to bed until late."

Trischi seemed surprised at the idea of the four pupils helping each other. "I see. I suppose this is about the zoo, isn't it?"

Luckily for Isy, she was saved from answering by the

---

dusty – staubig;
hesitant – zögernd;
to blush – erröten

sound of the bell. The pupils on the playground started moving in the same direction. Like a **flock** of impatient birds, they all pushed through the doors of the building. Isy could see Amanda talking to Tannhäuser and Jelly Baby. What were they planning?

Trischi turned towards the staff room. "I hope you're not trying to make headlines again!"

There was no doubt about it: he was referring to their last investigation! His memory was simply too good.

"Of course not!" Her answer was reassuring, if not entirely truthful. Isy hurried back to the classroom in time to hear their art teacher Mrs Müller-Märzdorf give a few words of advice before they set off for one of Berlin's most famous museums.

Class 7b marched to the train station. Thirty minutes later they arrived at the altar that gave the Pergamon Museum its name. It was huge! Whilst the rest of the class counted the steps to the **ancient** altar and listened to the thrilling story of its discovery, Isy took Amanda to one side. On their way there Amanda had fallen asleep on her shoulder whilst she'd chatted to the other girls. Now Isy wanted to know what her friend had been saying to Tannhäuser and Jelly Baby at breaktime.

"Oh yes," said Amanda, suddenly remembering. "They asked if you could bring the tape recorder to school tomorrow. They want to listen to the stranger's voice. Tannhäuser thinks they might recognize it."

That made sense. The two boys had spent plenty of time in the zoo. All the same, Isy wasn't sure that she

---

flock – Schwarm;
ancient – antik

wanted them to be involved. Just because the boys had helped them last night didn't mean they had a right to tell them what to do!

Mrs Müller-Märzdorf had told them that they could **sketch** whatever they liked in the museum, so they looked around inquisitively. Suddenly Amanda **dropped a bombshell.**

"Let's run away!" she **pleaded**. "We could disappear and come back after Easter. We need to escape from these gangsters!"

"Are you nuts?"

"We won't be able to get rid of them any other way."

"Where would we go though?"

"My cousin lives in Switzerland."

"But that would cost too much money!"

"We could always sell Monki to the travel agency."

"Oh don't start that again!" groaned Isy. "They only agreed to take him because they didn't have to pay. After Easter they'll be advertising trips to **Greenland**, and they won't need him any more!"

"Well, right now I just want to go to sleep!" said Amanda. "A museum bed would be fine. You can sketch me lying down on it. My back is killing me! I've never had to sleep on such an uncomfortable sofa! My mum still thinks I stayed at your place!"

"Ditto! But you won't find a bed in here. You're in the wrong museum!"

Isy knew her way around. Normally she liked museums. There was something special about those big airy

---

to sketch – skizzieren;
to drop a bombshell – hier: die Katze aus dem Sack lassen;
to plead – flehen;
Greenland – Grönland

rooms. People walked through them with quiet respect. Most of her classmates were looking at the exhibits in silent admiration – although they would never have admitted it, of course! They all remembered not to shout ... Except Hagen Golz, of course!

He was standing in front of an enormous historic gate, attempting to copy it on to his sketchpad. When he spotted them, he lowered his pad and waved at them.

"Hey! Over here!" Jelly Baby pointed to one of the museum attendants. "He won't believe that we've got these blue **tiles** at home!"

"At home?" Isy shook with laughter. "I don't think so! That's the Ishtar Gate! King Nebuchadnezzar built it. Those tiles are almost three thousand years old!"

Jelly Baby wasn't sure whether to believe her. "But our tiles are pretty old, too," he said in a small voice. Then he turned his attention back to his work.

Amanda finally seemed to have woken up a bit. She pointed energetically around the corner. "Maybe we should draw some of these!"

She was referring to a large collection of statues that filled the next room. They were sculptures of naked men.

"Come on, let's pick one!" Giggling, they dived in among the **nudes**.

On the way home it was Isy's turn to fall asleep on Amanda. It was only when the train pulled into their station that she slowly came back to life. "Were you asleep, too?" she asked her friend, who was folding up a newspaper with an air of disappointment.

---

tile – Kachel;
nude – Nackte/r

"No, I was reading this boring newspaper because I thought I might find something about Prince William's new girlfriend. Apparently, he hasn't got one! I'm going to put the paper in the **bin**!"

"Have you checked the advertisements?"

"Because of the Goth, you mean? I suppose you still believe in Father Christmas, too!"

Isy ignored her and picked up the **crumpled** newspaper. Amanda was already on her feet and heading for the door. "We're here!"

The train pulled noiselessly into their station. Two Vietnamese men had been smoking by the door. They jumped out, followed by Amanda. Isy grabbed her bag and left the carriage. Outside in the fresh air she stood still. For a moment she felt dazed, then she opened the paper again. She was convinced that Amanda didn't look carefully enough at the advertisements.

"Come on, I've got to get home!" her friend reminded her. Isy read the page. This time Amanda seemed to be right. There was nothing from the Goth.

Suddenly Isy stopped and stared. Printed on page four was a photo of a man wearing a black T-shirt, sitting in front of a computer. His face had been **pixelated** so no one could recognize him. The article was headed:

The man behind the scenes. Many famous crime writers are grateful to him for his helpful tips. "Super News" interviews F.B., Berlin's number one mafia specialist!

All of a sudden, Isy was completely awake. Amanda

---

bin – Abfall;
crumpled – zerknüllt;
to be pixelated – hier: unkenntlich gemacht sein

looked at her in astonishment as she carefully stowed the paper inside her bag.

"Why are you looking so surprised? Surely you don't expect me to throw away Berlin's number one mafia specialist? Especially not when he's Mr Rimpau's trusted friend ..."

– 13 –

The building looked completely **ordinary**, if not completely boring. It was obvious that only TV detectives had **sophisticated** glass offices that allowed you to see into all the other rooms.

The man at the desk didn't seem to be carrying a gun under his shirt either. There was nothing to suggest that he was a famous mafia expert.

"Is your name really F.B.?" Isy asked **doubtfully**.

The man stared at her through piercing blue eyes. "Of course not. Almost nothing in this room is real, girls." He held up his cup to the light. "Not even the coffee."

"So what should we call you then?"

"Whatever you like. Fred Baltruschat! Or Fabian Bauernöppel. Or Felix Bollerbusch ... Or maybe just Superintendent."

Was he being serious? Isy looked at Amanda in confusion, but her friend was staring at her shoelaces. She was probably still angry with Isy for making her come along.

"So you've been sent here by my old friend Rimpau, have you?" F.B. asked them again.

Isy nodded. She **avoided** his eyes. She was a terrible liar, as her parents had often told her.

---

ordinary – normal;
sophisticated – hier: schick;
doubtful – zweifelnd;
to avoid – vermeiden

"How is Rimpau anyway?"

"Very well. He told us that you sometimes help him with his books."

"Oh, I give him some background information every now and then. Writers aren't criminologists, you know. Well, what can I do for you?"

"I don't suppose you'll believe me, but we're being watched. It all started with our web report on the zoo." Isy stopped short. "Are you recording this conversation on tape?"

"On *two* tapes," he corrected her. Was he joking?

Isy was beginning to get the feeling that she'd been wrong. At first she'd thought that F.B. was as transparent as a pane of glass. But glass could create an illusion. Uncertainly, she told her story from beginning to end. To her frustration, she couldn't read F.B.'s expression. He looked as though he was listening to her, even when she'd finished.

"I don't suppose you believe me." Isy shuffled uncomfortably on her chair.

"I'm just thinking, that's all. Why don't you talk amongst yourselves? You could sing or something. You won't **disturb** me."

"What kind of music do you like?" Amanda asked inquisitively. "Do you prefer rap or Abba? Or maybe Heino? Then again, perhaps something grander is more your style. You know, like *I want to know what love is.*"

"My wife would tell you that I listen to Joe Cocker and nothing else. What makes you ask?"

"Because your **prickly pear** looks so unhealthy!"

---

to disturb – stören;
prickly pear – Feigenkaktus

Amanda stood up to take a better look at the dark green plant. "You should play it more Mexican music. A rumba perhaps. Heavy metal is bound to be bad for it. Last year one of our friends played Haydn to his **pumpkin**. He grew the biggest vegetable in Altgrünheide."

Isy couldn't understand why Amanda had mentioned Ruky. Ever since the autumn holidays they'd barely said a word about the good-looking half-Cuban with black **braids**. She hoped Amanda wasn't about to tell F.B. about his particular "talent" for breaking into other people's cars.

"Haydn, did you say?" The celebrated F.B. sat up in his chair. He no longer looked so friendly. "Well, I'd prefer a revolutionary march. But let's get back to your story. I must say I don't think it's especially polite of you to introduce yourself with a lie."

How had he found them out? Isy felt very small. She decided not to look at Amanda.

"My good friend Rimpau didn't send you here, and he certainly isn't feeling very well. He still hasn't recovered from his operation. While you were sitting in the waiting room, I made a few **enquiries**. We don't encourage thirteen-year-old girls to visit us, even if they are pretty."

"We saw your interview in the paper, and we thought you might be able to help us ..." Isy paused and changed her mind. "I mean, we thought the police might be interested in our findings. Last year we helped to catch a thief."

---

pumpkin – Kürbis;
braid – Zopf;
enquiry – Erkundigung

"I knew from the start that I was dealing with a pair of part-time detectives!" F.B. searched for a **match** to light his cigarette. "I suppose you like detective novels, too, right?"

"Amanda doesn't, but I love them!" said Isy. She told him her preference for classic English crime novels.

"Ah! Edgar Wallace and Agatha Christie!" sighed the superintendent, blowing blue rings of smoke into the air. "What I'd give to be solving a crime in one of those old wooden libraries, sat in front of an open fire, drinking a **vintage** glass of port."

"Or at the dinner-table, surrounded by solid silver candlesticks!" added Isy enthusiastically. "You could identify the **culprit** in the middle of his meal."

"I see we're on the same wavelength," F.B. said charmingly. "Did you bring the tape?"

Amanda looked up from her shoes. "We gave the tape to two friends. They thought they might be able to recognize the voice." She hesitated for a second. "Do you think we're in serious danger?"

"Danger? Not at all! In my opinion, there are too many stories in your story, and that's what makes it difficult to understand. But the mafia wouldn't get excited about a monkey!"

"The threat on the tape is real though," Isy objected. "Even Mr Rimpau thinks so."

"Mr Rimpau can think what he likes. I'm afraid I have to be more **cautious**."

"And then there's that business with Carrot," Amanda interrupted. "Don't you think it's funny that

---

match – Streichholz; vintage – alt;
culprit – Täter/in;
cautious – vorsichtig

he was attacked just when he was supposed to be meeting us?"

"Hmm, Carrot! That's another story that doesn't really seem to fit. *Robber-style Risotto*!" F.B. laughed dryly. "What was on the back of the recipe?"

"Some eggs in a nest."

"What kind of eggs?"

Isy smiled patiently. "Easter eggs, of course!"

"Did you bring the recipe with you?"

Amanda shook her head. "It's in my cook book."

"Fine. Well, I'll take care of Carrot as soon as he's back from the Maldives." F.B. looked at their disappointed faces. "Don't stare at me like that! I'd love to believe you, but in my opinion, things aren't quite the way they seem. Let me give you an example. You think the mafia is watching you. OK. Well, I can't say for certain that you're wrong – we're talking about organized crime, and you find that everywhere, so why not in the zoo? On the other hand, the most **recent** crimes in our zoos have been carried out by individual criminals, not by international smuggling rings. The criminals are very clever, of course. So far, we haven't been able to get hold of any proof."

"But you have your suspicions?" Isy's cheeks were red with excitement.

"Absolutely. That's not enough though." The expert obviously didn't like admitting that he'd failed. "In any case, I'm absolutely certain that no criminal, not even the mafia, would lie in wait every night, hoping to lock Isolde Schütze and Amanda Bornstein in a goat pen."

"What if it was a warning?" Isy **gulped**. Didn't he

---

recent – neueste/r, letzte/r;
to gulp – schlucken

understand how terribly frightened they'd been? Maybe he didn't believe them?

"Warnings don't work like that!" Rimpau's friend looked sceptical. "There has to be some other explanation. Think hard! Sometimes the answer is closer than you think."

At that moment the blue telephone started to ring. It was hidden under a mountain of paper. F.B. answered the call.

Isy took a sip of the lemonade that F.B.'s secretary had given them fifteen minutes earlier. Amanda's glass was empty already. She always drank everything in one gulp. What had the superintendent just said? There had to be another explanation. Huh, he didn't know anything at all! For him they were just two overenthusiastic part-time detectives who'd been imagining things in the zoo. Thank goodness he didn't know their nickname. The calamity queens ...

Building noise came in through the open window. The office was right next to the biggest construction site in Europe. The citizens of Berlin had renamed the area "**crane meadow**" because of the countless long-necked cranes. Last summer the machinery had danced to the rhythm of music conducted by Daniel Barenboim. The crane drivers had been worried that their steel giraffes would dance out of line, but they'd managed it all the same. The whole world had watched the spectacle on TV. It could only have happened in Berlin!

"What did you mean about there being another explanation?" asked Isy before the superintendent had

---

crane – Kran;
meadow – Wiese

put down the phone. "Do you think someone was **committing a crime** that night?"

"Maybe we prevented a **theft**," Amanda added hopefully. "Will we get a reward?"

"We can talk about that later." F.B. held out his hand towards them with a satisfied look on his face. "Give the tape to my secretary within the next few days and get back to your project. You wouldn't want someone else to win the prize, would you? Besides, I'm looking forward to my postcard from America!"

"So you really think we should carry on?" Amanda stared at the superintendent as though he'd told her to jump up and down in a cage full of vipers. "But it's so dangerous!"

"It's not dangerous, provided you go there during the official opening hours and keep to the official paths and only stick your noses where they belong. But if anything suspicious happens, don't hesitate to let me know!"

"I'm not telling him anything ever again!" declared Isy. They were standing in the elevator, on their way down. "I didn't come here to be laughed at!"

A **pickled gherkin** couldn't be sourer than Isy after their meeting with F.B. It had taken a lot of courage for them to visit Berlin's number one mafia specialist, and he had treated them like kids! That was the last time she **bothered** to cooperate with the police. With any luck, Tannhäuser and Jelly Baby had made more **progress** with the tape!

---

to commit a crime – ein Verbrechen begehen;
theft – Diebstahl;
pickled gherkin – Essiggurke;
to bother – hier: sich die Mühe machen;
progress – Fortschritt

– 14 –

The next day they met the boys in the bike shed at break-time. Tannhäuser and Jelly Baby had identified the stranger's voice.

"He works in the bird house!" muttered Tannhäuser, placing the cassette in Amanda's impatient hands.

"How do you know?"

"He speaks really softly. We started talking to him about the web project. He seems to know a lot about computers. By the way, we'll be at the zoo this afternoon. We can point him out to you if you like."

"What if he recognizes us?" asked Amanda in horror.

She was right. They couldn't let him see them. They would have to **disguise** themselves. When was the last time they'd disguised themselves? Everyone disguised themselves during carnival season, of course. When they were little, they used to dress up all the time. They'd wear their mums' wedding dresses and **ball gowns**. Standing in front of a full-length mirror, they used to experiment with handbags, make-up, hats and high-heeled shoes that were far too big for them. But that was a long time ago. This time their disguises had to be authentic. They weren't little kids any more.

The last period was Biology. Under the supervision of Mrs Schwammfuß, they used the **remains** of their

---

to disguise – verkleiden;
ball gown – Ballkleid;
remains – Reste

concentration to discover the differences between **composite** and **labiate flowers**. In the meantime Isy's imagination was busy disguising Amanda with sunglasses and a **plait**. As for herself, she would disguise her eyes with Chinese slits and spray her curls with Sassi's green hairspray.

Mrs Schwammfuß couldn't understand why Isolde had suddenly started to laugh. She had no idea that Isy was imagining herself with a lettuce on her head!

It wasn't until they were leaving the classroom that Isy had her best idea. She watched as her Turkish classmates put on their headscarves before they walked home. It was just as Mr Rimpau had said – the best ideas were out there; she only had to open her eyes.

They giggled continuously all the way to the bird house. Their Muslim disguise was enough to send them into fits of laughter. And best of all, no one could guess the reason for their amusement. On the train, on the street and in the zoo, everyone just saw two Turkish girls having fun. Their disguise was perfect.

The old woman with the grey bun was sitting on a bench near the antelope enclosure, knitting in the pale afternoon sun. She looked up in astonishment as they hurried past and shouted their usual greeting. She stared at them through her thick glasses.

"I nearly didn't recognize you!" she laughed, lowering her knitting for a moment. "Why the disguise?"

"We're supporting our Turkish classmates!" Amanda explained quickly as Isy tried not to laugh.

Tannhäuser and Jelly Baby were waiting outside the

---

composite flowers – Korbblütler;
labiate flowers – Lippenblütler;
plait – Zopf

birdhouse. They **wolf-whistled appreciatively** – until they realized that the Turkish beauties were really their classmates.

"Hello, brontosaurus!" Amanda gave Jelly Baby's bear-like **belly** a playful prod. "I didn't think you went for **veiled** ladies!"

They dived into the noisy world of chirps and feathers. The cages were filled with tropical and sub-tropical plants. Some of the birds were **dazzlingly** colourful, others were no more remarkable than **sparrows**, while some were more exotic than the most extraordinary flower.

Isy couldn't stop staring at the **golden-breasted starling**, with its violet feathers, turquoise head and yellow belly, while Amanda's mouth started watering at the sight of the **jambu fruit dove**. Its pale pink, white and cinnamon feathers reminded her of the creamy colours of a delicious **ice-cream sundae**.

Some birds had red eyes and green feet, while others had big hard **beaks** as black as **ebony**. The air was sticky and hot. Squeaks, squawks and chirps filled the cages like the soundtrack to a jungle movie. Isy saw Amanda wipe the sweat from her forehead. It was so

---

to wolf-whistle – hinterherpfeifen;
appreciative – anerkennend;
belly – Bauch;
veiled – verschleiert;
to dazzle – blenden;
sparrow – Spatz;
golden-breasted starling – Königsglanzstar;
jambu fruit dove – Jambo-Fruchttaube;
ice-cream sundae – Eisbecher;
beak – Schnabel;
ebony – Ebenholz

hot that she couldn't wait to take off her headscarf, but they still hadn't seen the man who had forced them to disguise themselves.

Tannhäuser came towards them. He had just finished his second **circuit**. He shook his head slightly.

"If they don't find him soon, we'll disappear in a puff of smoke!" Amanda muttered crossly. She stopped admiring the exotic birds and turned to the exotic vegetation. As usual she was attracted to the cactuses. With Argus eyes she searched among the baobabs and **poinsettias** for Aeschylus's prickly relatives, while Isy spoke softly into the microphone, dictating the information from the labels.

Their concentration was interrupted by the sound of a warning whistle. That was Jelly Baby! He was keeping watch outside the bird house. The man was obviously nearby. They rushed towards the door and nearly crashed into Tannhäuser. Jelly Baby ran towards them excitedly.

"He's in the children's zoo," he gasped. "He's feeding the ducks."

The children's zoo wasn't far from the bird house. Ponies, chickens, kid goats, **donkeys**, geese and ducks were kept there.

Nervously they joined the crowd of noisy preschool children who were impatiently waiting for a chance to stroke the animals. A man of medium height and strong build was leaning against the fence. His face was fleshy and his forehead was marked with a **wedge-shaped** scar. He had just thrown a bucket of bird seed

---

circuit – Rundgang;
poinsettia – Weihnachtsstern;
donkey – Esel; wedge-shaped – keilförmig

onto the floor and was smoking a cigarette while the birds gobbled up the food. He didn't seem dangerous, but he didn't necessarily look harmless either. Guys like that always appeared in detective stories. Sometimes they turned out to be criminals … Isy couldn't remember seeing him before. But that didn't mean that he hadn't seen her. Anyone who worked at the zoo would know all its secret hiding places and would be able to watch everything without being seen. Putting a face to the mysterious stranger was definitely progress.

"Let's go home now," Amanda whispered. She was too frightened to look at the man. "It's scary!"

"Don't be ridiculous!" Isy cried triumphantly. "It's not scary! Now we know who he is! Once we've found out what he's **up to**, we can hand him over to F.B.!"

"What do you think? Is he the one who attacked you?" Tannhäuser whispered behind them.

During their unexpected night in the cellar Isy and Amanda had told the boys some, but not all, of the story. Now Tannhäuser and Jelly Baby obviously expected to hear the rest.

"*Two* people attacked us. He might have been one of them. And Carrot was attacked by someone, too."

"Carrot?" echoed Jelly Baby. "That's a vegetable, not a name!"

"You've seen Carrot, remember! He's the one who was attacked last week. You were there when he was carried out of the nocturnal house."

"You mean the guy with the red hair? What's he got to do with you?"

"Amanda was supposed to be meeting him, but then he was attacked!"

---

to be up to sth – etwas vorhaben

Tannhäuser gave a low whistle. "Wow, you two are up to your ears in this business!"

"We know! But no one listens to us."

"We'll listen to you!" Jelly Baby **thumped his chest**. "Go on then, spit it out!" It sounded so funny that they all had to laugh.

Tannhäuser pointed towards the man at the fence. "Maybe we should go and talk to him. We could ask him if he'll help with our project."

The boys had sensed the opportunity for an adventure. They were desperate to **join in** the game of cops and robbers. But how could Amanda and Isy work together with their rivals?

"Think it over!" growled Jelly Baby when they didn't respond. He sounded disappointed. "The offer's open, but we won't wait forever."

They walked off. Isy still couldn't quite believe it. The brains of 7b and the class clown: it was such an odd pair! What did they see in each other?

Amanda cast a nervous look towards the frightening figure who'd been **haunting** her dreams. "We should accept their help. We can't watch everyone at once!"

"Who else are you planning to watch then?"

"I've noticed something." Amanda looked around carefully to make sure no one was listening. They were surrounded by excitable little kids. "She can't knit!"

"Who can't knit?"

"The old woman! The one with the bun."

Isy was speechless. Her friend continued in a **confident** tone, "I noticed it a while ago. She pretends to

---

to thump one's chest – sich in die Brust werfen;
to join in – mitmachen bei;
to haunt – herumspuken in; confident – selbstsicher

knit, but she's not doing anything. She's still on the same row!"

"Maybe she can't see properly. Her glasses are awfully thick!"

Amanda shook her head. "In that case, she should be able to see perfectly! Anyway, I haven't seen her do a single proper **stitch** – and I should know!"

That was true. When Amanda first joined their class, she used to knit during lessons. It was only when Trischi asked her to knit a **ribbed** polo-neck sweater for him that she wisely decided to stop. Where knitting was **concerned**, Amanda was an expert.

"Why would she pretend to knit?" Isy asked in confusion. The answer was already taking shape in her brain. Maybe the woman was no more harmless than she and Amanda were Turkish.

"Wow!" she said decisively. "If you're right, I'll make you my first criminological assistant!"

---

stitch – Masche, Stich;
ribbed – gerippt;
to concern – betreffen

– 15 –

There was a **persistent** splashing noise when Isy woke up the next day. At first she thought it was the sound of a nice, hot shower, but then she looked out of the window and realized her mistake. This certainly wasn't the weather for a trip to the zoo. Luckily, that wasn't on the agenda anyway. Amanda had an appointment with Dr Rosi after school, and Isy had agreed to go with her.

Isy got out of bed and followed the smell of cake. She looked into the kitchen and spotted a cake tin behind the transparent oven door. Of course! Her mother was expecting visitors that afternoon. She was planning to show her collection of plastic containers to some former colleagues. With any luck, the afternoon would lead to some lively conversation and to some good business as well. Last night Isy's mum had started to prepare a bowl of peach punch – it tasted delicious!

"How did the film end?" Isy asked as she came out of the bathroom and joined her parents for breakfast.

"It was all a bit confusing," her mum said. "Your father went to sleep!"

Isy's dad was reading the sports section of the paper. He looked up. "There were too many **red herrings**! No one could have known who the murderer was. It was completely unrealistic!"

---

persistent – andauernd;
red herring – falsche Fährte

"Actually," said Isy **knowledgeably**, "it's just the same in real life." She took a bite out of her toast. "Trust me!"

There were only two topics of conversation at school that day. Firstly Saskia had dyed her hair honey-blonde, which made her look completely different; and secondly someone had pinned a picture of Philadelphia to the wall. The photo wasn't helping 7b's concentration. Soon they were all wondering who the lucky winners would be. One fortunate group would see the city for itself. The class kept glancing hopefully at the photo. Isy found it hard not to stare, too.

Two of their lessons were cancelled because the teachers had the flu. As soon as school was over, Isy and Amanda walked hand in hand towards Dr Rosi's dental practice. Half of 7b seemed to be waiting for an appointment. The chairs in the little waiting room were occupied by Richard, Jens and Jelly Baby. Vanessa and Jennifer were there, too. Jennifer was having a birthday party on Tuesday and had invited some of the girls in 7b. A **drilling** noise was coming from Dr Rosi's room.

"Where is your **bosom buddy**?" Amanda asked Jelly Baby. She sat down next to him on the last available chair. "I thought you two never left each other's side!"

Jelly Baby looked pale. He pointed towards the drilling noise. It seemed to be making him nervous. Vanessa and Jennifer didn't look particularly confident

---

knowledgeable – bewandert;
to drill – bohren;
bosom buddy – Busenfreund

either, even though Dr Rosemarie Schlei was known for being nice. All the schoolkids liked and trusted her because she didn't mind telling them that she was scared of visiting the dentist, too. Besides, she was pretty. She had blonde hair, kind eyes, and an energetic receptionist by the name of Mrs Zahn.

Isy loved sweets and was sometimes too lazy to clean her teeth at night. On this occasion she was sitting in the waiting room calmly – but that was only because she didn't have to go in. Amanda, on the other hand, was staring fearlessly at Dr Rosi's door. Eventually it opened and Tannhäuser came out, smiling and looking embarrassed. Before anyone else could move, Amanda jumped up and disappeared inside. It was actually Jelly Baby's turn, but he stayed on his chair and sighed in relief.

"I'll wait outside," Tannhäuser told him and walked off with rounded shoulders. Isy followed him out of the waiting room.

Reginald Häuser was in the car park, playing football with an empty beer can. He kicked it between the cars and through the **puddles**.

"I've got more news for you!" Isy called out to him and told him about the friendly old woman. She had a suggestion: if the boys were happy to find out about the man from the bird house, she and Amanda would watch the old lady.

"After all, she might be involved in the affair," said Isy.

"You bet! There's no reason why old people can't be criminals, too." There was a rattling noise as he kicked the beer can into the bushes. "Anyone can be a spy.

---

puddle – Pfütze

Maybe she wants extra money to top up her pension. Some grannies even rob banks."

"She might do it to keep herself amused," suggested Isy. "She seems an interesting type of person."

Tannhäuser frowned. He usually used that expression when he was solving problems on the blackboard. "Fine: Hagen and I will follow the guy with the quiet voice, and you two will make the granny sing."

"Sing?" echoed Amanda, who had **crept up** on them in the dark. "Why do you want us to make her sing?"

"I want to know whether she's working for someone, and who that someone might be."

"What if she's a harmless old woman?" Amanda looked worried. She clearly wished that she'd never told Isy of her suspicion. "The fake knitting might just be a funny **habit**."

Isy shook her head. "She's too **bright** to be mad. I'd say she's not the type for knitting."

"Just like you!" Amanda laughed.

Tannhäuser glanced at his watch. He had to go to his cello lesson. "Where shall we meet?"

"At Amanda's," Isy said without thinking. "She's got plenty of room, haven't you, Amanda?"

"Why does it always have to be me?" her friend growled. But she didn't seem to mind.

Isy couldn't wait to get home. She loved to see the kitchen full of people, with everyone chatting happily around a table full of food. The cake had looked truly delicious ...

---

to creep up – heranschleichen;
habit – Angewohnheit;
bright – hier: klug

She ran up the steps and turned her key in the front door. There was an awkward silence in the house. The guests had disappeared. How disappointing. She put on her slippers and hung her coat on its **hook**. Selma walked up to her and rubbed her furry head against her knee.

"What's wrong, Selma?" Isy whispered. "Why has everyone gone?"

Her mother was washing up. She was surrounded by dirty dishes and the remains of the party. Isy gave her an energetic kiss.

"How was it? Did you sell much?"

"Sell much?" Her mother sounded sad. "I didn't sell anything at all. But at least they found it funny."

"Found what funny?"

"Me!"

"You don't mean that, do you?" Isy gazed unhappily at the colourful containers that her mother had piled up on the counter – a whole pyramid of "cheese castles', "cucumber elevators" and "salad pavilions".

"They weren't laughing at you," she said **firmly**, "they were laughing at all these stupid names. I'd laugh, too, if I were them."

"Well, Mum threw them out!" Benedikt announced. He had appeared in the doorway. "I don't **blame** her!"

"I didn't throw them out," his mother corrected him. "I just ended the party a little earlier than expected. Not so long ago I used to be their boss. And now here I am, trying to sell them cheese castles ..." She fell silent. "I expect I would have found it funny, too."

---

hook – Haken;
firm – fest, hier: überzeugt;
to blame – beschuldigen

"Have you told Grandma about it?" Isy asked. Her mum nodded. "Well?" Isy continued. "What did she say?"

"Oh, you know your grandma. *It's no use crying over* ***spilt*** *milk*!"

"Well, she's right, you know!" Benedikt leaned towards the cake and stole the biggest slice. "Can I have some punch?"

"Forget the punch!" Isy said angrily. "Stop eating, and tell Mum what to do!"

"I've told her already! She needs to go on a computer course!"

"All the courses are fully booked."

The plates rattled in their mother's hands. The Schützes' **stone-age** household didn't even have a dishwasher. Amanda had been horrified when she first came round to visit.

Isy was surprised by her mother's tone of voice. Was she sorry that she couldn't do the course? Maybe she was ready to learn computing after all. There was hope for her yet. Isy helped herself to some cake and disappeared into her bedroom. She started to do her homework. A few minutes later she found herself in Benedikt's room. He was doing his homework, too.

"Maybe you should teach Mum how to use a computer. I think she wants to learn."

"We don't have a computer! I can't use the kitchen scales, you know!"

He was right. The idea wouldn't work without a computer. She should have thought of that.

Isy was about to go back to her room when she was

---

to spill – verschütten;
stone-age – steinzeitlich

distracted by the television. The picture showed a magnificent palace and a group of Arabs in long white robes. As the reporter explained, the men were waiting to see the sheikh. Isy was mainly interested in the fact that some of the men were holding birds of prey. The birds had large beaks and were sitting on **cushions** that were tied to the men's arms. Isy giggled. Did people in the Middle East take falcons for a walk instead of dogs?

"They're northern falcons," Benedikt explained. "You'll never believe how much they're worth."

"How much then?"

"A trained falcon can fetch a quarter of a million dollars. A **gyrfalcon** costs even more."

"You can't be serious!"

"Have you ever seen them hunting?" Benedikt's face took on a dreamy look. "A **Peregrine falcon swoops** on its **prey** at 300 kilometres per hour. It's more exciting than any of your detective stories! People in the Middle East love them. Falcons are a kind of status symbol there. Those guys would happily pay that much for them."

"How do you know all this?"

Benedikt was forced to admit that he'd seen the documentary once before.

Isy was still in shock when she sat down at her desk. A quarter of a million dollars for a single bird! Unbelievable ... Just wait until she told Amanda. Her friend would explode with rage when she realized that she'd been left with Monki instead of a gyrfalcon!

---

cushion – Kissen;
gyrfalcon – Gerfalke;
Peregrine falcon – Wanderfalke;
to swoop – sich stürzen;
prey – Beute

– 16 –

With the exception of Christmas, Easter was Isy's favourite festival. She was really looking forward to searching Granny Dora's garden for Easter eggs. She knew that she'd find colourful chocolate bunnies in the **juniper** bushes and a detective novel at the foot of the old **pear** tree.

As soon as the Easter egg hunt had finished, the family would sit down to a traditional Easter breakfast in Granny Dora's cottage. They'd have a home-made **bread plait** and hard-boiled eggs that had been dyed with onion skins. It was the same every year, and this year would be no different.

Amanda's family had their own way of doing things. Ever since they'd moved to Berlin, they celebrated Easter with relatives in Nuremberg. Amanda had to hunt for her Easter eggs among armchairs and cushions, while her father ate hard-boiled eggs cooked in red wine.

The long-awaited holidays were only a week away, and Amanda would be off to her birthplace in the south. It was time to remind Mr Knöpfle of his promise. Isy leaned forwards decisively and picked up the phone.

---

juniper – Wacholder; pear – Birne;
bread plait – Hefezopf

Two days later Isy and Amanda were walking triumphantly over the forbidden maintenance area in the company of Mr Knöpfle. The zoologist didn't know it, but he was taking them exactly where they wanted to go.

The two girls kept an eye out for the green crates while Mr Knöpfle showed them around the mysterious maintenance buildings, which weren't mysterious at all. They simply contained a few rooms and a **sick bay** for the workers. There was a sick bay for the animals, too.

"Where are the crates?" Isy asked suddenly as they walked over to the loading ramp. There was no sign of them. She had turned on the tape recorder when Mr Knöpfle wasn't watching. "You know, those crates with '*Live Animals!*' written on the side."

The zoologist glanced around. "The crates for live animals? I guess there haven't been any **deliveries** today."

"What kind of deliveries do you mean?" Isy was trying to sound casual in the hope that Mr Knöpfle wouldn't notice her excitement. "We want to know *everything*!"

The zoologist gave a friendly **nod**. "Well, we usually get live mice and rats – they're tasty **treats** for our lions!" He realized that Amanda was pulling a face, so he added that lorry-loads of fruit and vegetables were unloaded from the fruit farms, too. After all, the zoo had thirteen thousand animals to feed!

So there was nothing odd about the green crates after

---

sick bay – Krankenstation;
delivery – Lieferung;
nod – Nicken;
treat – hier: Leckerbissen

all, Isy thought in disappointment. Then Mr Knöpfle suggested that they paid a visit to the kitchens to see what was cooking. They walked into a building next to the ramp, where a dozen huge saucepans were boiling on an enormous **stove**.

"Do you really cook for the animals?" Amanda asked, lifting the lid of one of the pans. She sniffed the contents. "Rice and **raisins**!" she exclaimed. "Cool!"

"It's not exactly traditional Swabian cooking, I suppose." Mr Knöpfle laughed. "The monkeys like it though." He said hello to the cook.

"I'm just showing the girls around," he explained. "They're working on a school project."

"What would you like to know?" the cook asked them, handing Amanda a spoon. "Want to taste?"

"Sure!" Amanda **bravely** ate a spoonful of monkey food. "Needs a bit more salt," she announced.

"Not for animals, it doesn't," the cook reassured her. "We feed the rice cake to monkeys and birds. They'd get thirsty if we added more salt."

"Do you know what an elephant eats in a day then?" Isy asked inquisitively. She pointed the tape recorder in the direction of the cook.

"You bet I do!" The cook nodded. "On a good day an elephant will consume thirty kilos of hay, twenty-five kilos of straw, twenty-five kilos of **turnips**, two buckets of **feed**, one bucket of carrots, six **stale** loaves of bread, some extra fruit and vegetables, and a bath-

---

stove – Herd;
raisin – Rosine;
brave – mutig;
turnip – Rübe;
feed – hier: Kraftfutter;
stale – altbacken

tub of water … In winter they eat the Christmas trees that don't end up in people's houses."

"Sounds just like what you eat for breakfast, Amanda!" Isy **teased** her.

All of a sudden, the spoon fell noisily to the floor. Amanda looked as though she'd seen a ghost. She was staring at Carrot, who was standing at the door. The zoologist seemed surprised to see him, too. The next moment Patrick Talke had vanished.

"Carrot!" shouted Amanda. "Hey, Carrot! Wait for me!"

Without stopping to think, she ran after him. Isy followed her outside. The maintenance area was shining brightly with March sunshine. There was no one in sight. A few sparrows were fighting over some food, and a **dandelion** stuck its head above the stone floor. Carrot had disappeared.

"He'll be in the monkey house!" shouted Isy. She raced ahead, while Amanda followed more slowly behind her.

"I thought … I'd … uh … seen a ghost!" she gasped.

They were out of luck. According to his workmates, Patrick Talke had gone home already. Feeling completely **discouraged**, they set off home.

On the way to the exit they kept an eye out for the old woman. Ever since they'd decided to question her, she seemed to have vanished from the face of the earth. They couldn't go back to the kitchens now. Not after they'd abandoned Mr Knöpfle so rudely. What a mess.

---

to tease sb – jmdn. ärgern;
dandelion – Löwenzahn;
discouraged – entmutigt

"He ran away as soon as I saw him," Amanda said in a sad voice. "You didn't have to follow me, Isy!"

"So it's my fault now, is it?" Isy protested **indignantly**. "You ran off like some kind of mad monkey. What was I supposed to do? Stay behind with a saucepan of rice? Besides, we absolutely have to talk to Carrot."

"I know!"

"I guess we both agree on that then," Isy said. She didn't want to argue with her friend. "We'll have to **apologize** to Mr Knöpfle though. We'll tell him that you suddenly felt sick."

Amanda nodded. "But what are we going to do about Carrot?"

"We'll catch up with him at home."

"At home? You don't even know where he lives!"

"No, but I know where we can find a phone box. We'll look up his address."

Finding a telephone book wasn't as easy as they'd hoped. The **directory** had been stolen from the first phone box, and an impatient queue was waiting outside the second phone box while a pale girl talked for ages on the phone.

"Why don't we look up the address at home?" suggested Amanda. "We can use my dad's computer. You can find anything on D-Info."

Amanda was absolutely right. They placed a silvery disk in the CD drive and got rid of Mrs Bornstein, who kept trying to help. After a few clicks Patrick Talke's phone number and address appeared on the screen.

---

indignant – empört;
to apologize to sb – sich bei jmdm. entschuldigen;
directory – Telefonbuch

They were pleased to see that he lived close to an underground station. Carrot's eyes would be as round as **saucers** when he saw them!

They knocked and waited in anticipation. His eyes weren't *quite* as round as saucers, but he did look very surprised.

"What do you want?" he asked in bewilderment, standing in the doorway and blocking their entry. He obviously didn't intend to invite them in. "I didn't ask you to visit me, did I?"

"We're so pleased that you're OK again!" purred Amanda. "We thought you were dead at first!"

"Well, now you can see I'm alive," he said coolly. "And in order to stay that way, I have to eat – which was what I was doing until you interrupted me!"

"What's on the menu?" Isy asked in a friendly voice. "Not robber-style risotto, I hope?"

Carrot's pale, **freckled** face turned a faint shade of pink. "Like I said, I'm busy."

He took a step backwards into the hall and tried to close the door, but Isy's foot got there first. The door bounced off her foot and opened again.

"Do you want me to have you arrested for **harassment**?" the zoo keeper hissed angrily. "I expect you're the ones who set the police on to me. Well, thanks a million!"

"Has F.B. been talking to you? Don't worry, he hasn't got a clue."

"That's not the impression he gave me. Now beat it!"

---

saucer – Untertasse;
freckled – sommersprossig;
harassment – Belästigung

"Not until you tell us what the recipe means!"

"What recipe?" asked Carrot, pretending not to understand.

Isy looked at his brightly coloured shirt. How could they ever have mistaken him for a Goth?

"You know exactly what I'm talking about – the scrap of paper that you were holding when we found you."

"I don't want anything more to do with it, OK?"

"We were attacked a few days ago, too, you know. You're not the only one."

Carrot looked at them in surprise. "Really?"

"They tied us up and locked us in a goat pen!"

"All right then." Carrot was breathing heavily. "The scrap of paper was a clue. But if you're too dumb to read it, you may as well forget it."

The door slammed shut. The noise made them jump. Isy hammered on the door.

"You could at least tell us about the man in the bird house! You know, the one with the scar!"

"Do you mean Tengelmann? He came to the zoo a few weeks ago." Carrot's voice sounded as though he was standing right behind the door. "He used to work in the zoo in East Berlin. He's writing an article on birds in **captivity**. Why do you want to know?"

"Because his voice was on our tape!"

"Your tape? I don't know what you're talking about. Take my advice: you should **mind your own business**!"

They heard the sound of another door slamming

---

captivity – Gefangenschaft;
to mind one's own business – sich um seinen eigenen Kram kümmern

inside the flat. Carrot was gone. They walked down the steps in disappointment. Amanda pulled a face. She looked as though she had toothache.

"He's such a **coward**!" she snorted. "He definitely hasn't been to the Maldives, you know! He isn't tanned at all!"

"He's just scared, Amanda. Someone attacked him, remember? He's not really a coward."

"The criminals weren't exactly nice to us either," her friend grumbled. She opened the heavy door on the ground floor of the building. As they stepped outside, there was a bitter smell of smoke. Isy had smelt that kind of smoke before in Granny Dora's garden. The gardeners in the nearby **allotments** must be having a spring-clean and burning old leaves.

"He's probably cross with us because he thinks we set the police on to him," Isy explained. "But at least we've found out Mr Tengelmann's name. Now all we need to do is solve the puzzle of the recipe. We'll have to look in your cook book and study it word for word. We're not as dumb as Carrot thinks!"

"I still don't see how it can be a clue!" Amanda protested. "*Use fifty grammes of rice per person.* I mean, does that sound like a hidden message to you?"

"We'll soon find out!"

In the end, they weren't able to find out anything at all. They searched, sweated and **cursed**, but no matter how many times they looked through Amanda's cook book, the recipe had gone.

---

coward – Feigling;
allotment – Schrebergarten;
to curse – fluchen

– 17 –

Jennifer Niemann's thirteenth birthday party was on Tuesday afternoon. Isy and Amanda weren't exactly best friends with her, but they went all the same. Sassi and Bini were going and, besides, Jennifer's parties were always full of surprises. One year they'd set off in a minibus for an amusement park, and another year they'd visited a circus. There was bound to be another adventure this year.

School finished, and an hour later they met up again at Jenni's flat. They put two presents on the table: some writing paper with hearts on it and the latest Spice Girls CD.

The guests were made up of some of Jennifer's classmates, plus two of her aunts and her cousin Berni. Once everyone had arrived, Jennifer's grandma helped her mum to hand out paper crowns and colourful **badges**. The guests were led into a minibus where Jenni's father was waiting at the wheel.

Isy and Amanda slid on to a seat behind Saskia and Binette. They were looking forward to finding out where the birthday trip would be taking them. It was about time they did something different!

"Is everyone on board?" Mr Niemann asked, and they all shouted, "Yes!" The minibus set off. Jennifer's mother was carrying a large bag of prizes. She pulled out the star prize. It was a video tape of the *Lion King*.

---

badge – Button

As always they had to guess the first letter of their **destination**. The party food would be waiting for them there.

Last March Sassi had won the star prize: a Tic Tac Toe CD.

They all started shouting letters of the alphabet. Suddenly Isy had a terrible suspicion. By the time Jennifer's cousin had yelled out "z", she knew she was right. Berni won the video. Isy could hardly believe it.

"You know where we're going, don't you?" she whispered to Amanda.

"You can't be serious!" her friend groaned. She tried not to listen while Jenni's mum explained that this year's party would be held at the zoo. Mrs Niemann was very **cheerfully**.

Everyone agreed, but two of the guests said nothing, staring silently out of the window.

Mr Niemann parked the bus at the lion gate, and they all moved noisily in the direction of the café where the birthday cake would be served. Most of the other guests hadn't been to the zoo for ages, so they took the opportunity to look around.

Isy and Amanda followed slowly behind them with sour expressions on their faces. They could only hope that they wouldn't bump into Tannhäuser and Jelly Baby while they were wearing their idiotic paper hats.

They were lucky. They managed to get to the restaurant without anyone recognizing them, and they sat down for the birthday **feast**. The table was decorated

---

destination – Ziel;
cheerful – fröhlich;
feast – Festmahl

with flowers, candles and a choice of mouth-watering cakes. Isy spotted a **pineapple** cake, a Black Forest **Gateau**, and a cheesecake. Mrs Niemann helped a waitress to fill the guests' cups with coffee or hot chocolate. Isy asked for a slice of cheesecake, while Amanda wanted pineapple. Berni sat opposite them, biting his nails. He looked embarrassed to be the only boy among a party of giggling, chatting girls. Jennifer's other male cousin, Klausi, was in bed with the flu. He hadn't been able to come.

Mr Niemann circled the table, filming the celebration with a camcorder. Just as they were about to start eating, a familiar voice asked for the bill. The person was sitting at the table behind them. Isy was so surprised that her fork stopped in mid-air. Amanda froze, too. They looked at each other. It was too risky to turn round. The old woman hadn't recognized them because of their paper hats.

They heard her say a few words to the waitress, then there was a rattling of **coins**, and a chair scraped backwards. The old woman walked slowly out of the room. What were they to do? They could stay at the table and finish their cake, or run after her.

Let's stay here and eat cake, Amanda's eyes begged her.

"This is our only chance!" hissed Isy. "She can't get away from us now!" She dragged Amanda out of her chair. They promised Mrs Niemann that they'd be back soon.

"I don't see why we couldn't eat our cake!" growled Amanda. They fetched their coats. In no time Isy was

---

pineapple – Ananas; gateau – Torte;
coin – Münze

out of the door and watching the figure disappear in the direction of the bird house.

"What did I tell you?" she said. "She's involved in this as well. I bet she's on her way to meet up with Tengelmann."

They followed their suspect, taking care to stick close to the bushes and trees. Soon the truth **emerged**. Isy had guessed right: the old woman went into the bird house and glanced around.

"Pretend that we're here **by chance**," Isy said, taking off her paper crown. "Don't say a word about seeing her in the restaurant."

"OK, Miss Superintendent!" growled Amanda, putting her hat in her bag. "But let's hurry! I can't wait to taste that pineapple cake!"

They walked into the bird house, and everything went just as Isy had hoped. They found the old lady outside a cage full of **roadrunners**. They pretended to spot her by chance. The grey-haired woman didn't suspect anything. She made a few friendly enquiries about the progress of their project, and the two girls told her about their visit to the kitchens. Throughout the entire conversation Isy was waiting for the moment when she could voice her suspicions. She knew from detective stories that it was best to take the culprit by surprise. The aim was to shock the criminal into making a confession. She finally saw her opportunity when they all sat down on a bench. The old woman broke a bar of chocolate into three pieces. Isy saw her knitting needles shining in her bag.

---

to emerge – hier: sich herausstellen;
by chance – zufällig;
roadrunner – Rennkuckuck

"I guess you like knitting then?" she shouted, trying to make herself heard above the squawking and chirping from the aviary. They were sitting next to some particularly noisy birds.

"These days I only knit for my grandchildren. Sweaters and scarves are always useful, you know."

"What are you knitting at the moment?"

"A little jacket for my youngest grandson."

"I know it sounds rude, but my friend thinks you can't knit. She says you're pretending. Isn't that right, Amanda?"

Amanda had just put a piece of chocolate in her mouth. She blushed.

Isy studied the woman's expression, but she didn't **bat an eyelid**. In fact, her friendly smile stayed perfectly in place. She could have been smiling for a photo. Isy's shock tactics didn't appear to have worked. Either the woman was completely harmless or very dangerous indeed.

"What a strange thing to say! Why would I do that?" The old lady shook her head in astonishment.

"Perhaps you're trying to hide your real intentions!" Isy said bravely. She was determined not to be too soft. Real detectives couldn't let themselves feel sorry for their suspects. It wasn't easy all the same.

"My intentions? What kind of intentions would I possibly want to hide?" Her eyes blinked at Isy in confusion from behind her pink-rimmed glasses. "Is this some kind of game? I hope it isn't a hidden camera programme! I've seen programmes like that on TV!" She looked around brightly.

Isy suddenly had a horrible feeling that she may

---

to not bat an eyelid – nicht mit der Wimper zucken

have gone too far. Amanda looked horrified. Should she give in? Apologize? Explain everything? Or try one last time to force a confession?

"You're meeting someone here, aren't you?" she said softly. "We know who it is. You're making a mistake, you know. The man's a criminal. Maybe it's not too late for you to change your mind. Go to the police! At your age they're bound to be nice to you – just plead **diminished responsibility**!"

The old woman finally lost her patience. "I'm not meeting anyone, and I'm perfectly responsible, thank you very much! After all this talking, I certainly need my heart tablets and a glass of water! I can't remember the last time I heard such nonsense!" She picked up her leather shopping bag and got to her feet. "Have you two been taking drugs or something?" She looked at them suspiciously. "You usually seem quite normal!" She disappeared angrily in the direction of the toilets.

"Congratulations, Miss Superintendent!" Amanda said dryly. "Now she'll probably have a heart attack."

Isy looked embarrassed. "The police do it all the time," she defended herself. "You're supposed to take the suspect by surprise. It always works in films ..."

"Well, I prefer love films. At least they don't teach you how to be rude to other people!" Amanda said **pointedly**.

It was all very well for her to say that. She was the one who'd suggested that the woman was a fake, and now she was refusing to take any of the blame.

"You said she couldn't knit, remember?" Isy accused her.

---

diminished responsibility – verminderte Zurechnungsfähigkeit; pointed – spitz

"Well, she can't! But that doesn't mean she's a criminal."

Isy fell silent. There was no answer to that. She could feel her heart beating as she waited for the woman to return. She would apologize straightaway. Maybe the old woman would forgive her once she told her what the zoo was really like. Isy glanced impatiently at the door to the toilets. By now a whole string of women had been in and out, but the old lady hadn't walked past. Maybe Isy's claims had really upset her? Perhaps she was feeling ill.

Amanda was staring at the toilet door, too. Isy could tell that she was thinking about pineapple cake. Amanda wouldn't let her forget this in a hurry! The birds in the aviary started squawking noisily again. Isy was getting worried. She stood up.

"I'm going to take a look!" she told Amanda. "Maybe she needs help."

She hurried along the corridor and pulled open the door to the toilets. The room was empty, as were all the **cubicles**. She looked around in disbelief. How was that possible? Where had the old woman got to?

Amanda's blonde head appeared around the door. "Isy?"

"She's gone!"

"What do you mean, *gone*?"

"Disappeared! Vanished! Just *gone*." Isy was so excited that she was gasping for breath. "You were absolutely right! And my shock tactics worked, too!"

"She wasn't knitting for her grandchildren!" Amanda shook her head. "She was lying all the time! But how did she get out? We were watching the door all the time."

---

cubicle – Kabine

"She definitely didn't leave through the door."

"Then she must have climbed out of a window."

"But there aren't any windows."

"What?" Amanda stared at her. "But she can't have disappeared into thin air!"

"Well, no," said Isy, bending down to **crawl** beneath the sinks. She didn't find what she was looking for, so she turned her attention to the basket full of crumpled paper towels. After searching around for a while, she waved something in the air. It was grey and curly. When Amanda looked at it more closely, it turned out to be a **wig**. She listened to Isy's explanation: "The old woman *did* walk out through that door – but she left as someone else!"

---

to crawl – krabbeln;
wig – Perücke

– 18 –

"That's the last time I invite either of you to my party!" Jennifer Niemann told them in a **wounded** voice. They had been trying to say sorry to her. "My mum says you're really rude."

"We had our reasons," Amanda said, trying to explain. "But we're not allowed to tell you."

"I suppose you were caught up in another robbery or something," Jennifer said in a cutting voice. "Well, I guess I should have known better than to invite a pair of calamity queens like you."

"The only **calamity** was your cake. It gave us **food poisoning**!" Isy snapped. She turned her back and walked off with Amanda.

"What? What was wrong with my cake?" Jennifer yelled after them aggressively. "It tasted fine to me!"

"If you like salmonella with pineapple, I guess!" Amanda rolled her eyes. "Your parties are a health risk!"

Jennifer started crying with rage and had to be **comforted** by Sassi and Bini. They all started whispering. Sassi pointed to Isy, Amanda, Tannhäuser and Jelly Baby. What was going on?

They found out when Sassi and Bini **launched** into

---

wounded – gekränkt;
calamity – Unglück, hier: Katastrophe;
food poisoning – Lebensmittelvergiftung;
to comfort – trösten;
to launch – beginnen, starten

an old classic. *It's so easy to fall in love, it's so easy to fa-a-all in love!* they sang, before bursting into collective laughter.

Were all their classmates that stupid?

During their first lesson that morning Isy decided to write a letter to Jenni. If Jennifer would take back what she'd said about calamity queens, Isy would take back her comments about the cake. The letter was passed from bench to bench towards the back of the class. Amanda sighed with relief and added her signature. She had been feeling **guilty** as well. In her view, they hadn't been entirely fair to Jennifer. After all, she had invited them to her party.

The answer came back as a tiny ball of paper. It dropped into Isy's lap while Trischi's back was turned. Jennifer was obviously keen to be friends again.

Isy opened her airmail. It wasn't from Jenni at all. Tannhäuser was suggesting a meeting at Amanda's flat **ASAP**.

That's **handy**, thought Isy. She'd been intending to suggest the same thing. The boys would be speechless when they found out what had happened to them the previous day in the bird house! She scribbled "15:00" on the scrap of paper and returned it **by the same means**.

"Sometimes I ask myself," said Trischi, who was still writing on the blackboard, "whether I work in a school or a post office." Once again he had proven that teachers have eyes in the backs of their heads.

---

guilty – schuldig;
ASAP (as soon as possible) – so bald wie möglich;
handy – praktisch;
by the same means – auf demselben Weg

After school Isy went back to Amanda's flat, and Hagen and Reginald turned up at the appointed time.

"We've got a big surprise for you!" Jelly Baby **boasted** as he crashed down into Amanda's blue armchair. "We've found out the name of the whisperer!"

"Is it Mr Tengelmann, by any chance?" Isy said proudly. "Well, we've got a big surprise for you, too!"

"Go on then," Jelly Baby demanded, pretending not to be impressed.

"We know who he's working with!"

"Who?" asked Tannhäuser, but Isy shook her head.

"We don't know her name ... but we do have her scalp!"

The boys' jaws dropped as they listened to what had happened in the bird house.

"That's completely mad!" Jelly Baby said in astonishment as Amanda waved the wig beneath his nose. "No one can tell what she looks like now!"

"We've thought long and hard about it," said Isy. "We couldn't understand how she had slipped through the net. We should have recognized the clothes she was wearing – but she probably turned her coat inside-out as well."

Tannhäuser was doing something on Amanda's PC. He seemed to be impressed by their news. "She must have been wearing the wig to make her look older," he guessed. "Which means she's probably younger than we thought. And I was sure we were fighting a criminal grandma!"

"She can't walk very well though," Amanda objected.

"She could be faking that, too." Isy remembered the

---

to boast – prahlen

woman's bright-sounding voice. "She's of medium height and she's slim. She must be quite sporty and strong. How else could she have attacked us in the zoo?"

"Are you saying that she and Tengelmann ...?" Amanda shook her head. "But she was always so nice to us."

"That's what you think!" said Jelly Baby, who was staring at the wall above Amanda's bed. A giant poster of Prince William smiled shyly into the room. "All that time she was spying on you **cold-bloodedly**. Do you remember what colour her eyes were?"

"How could we? She always wore thick glasses."

"So the culprit might be any of the women in the zoo!" Tannhäuser said in disappointment. "Let's focus on Tengelmann instead."

"But we can't prove anything!" Isy sighed. "We don't even know what they're planning to steal."

"You could steal practically anything if you wanted to."

"Are you trying to tell me that you could smuggle a rhino out of the zoo?" Amanda sounded unconvinced.

"If I put my mind to it, yes! It would be better to do it at night-time, of course."

"I suppose you'd lift it over the fence, tie a rope around its neck and walk it down the street?"

Tannhäuser gave a superior smile. "I'd just take out a few fence posts. My boat would be waiting on the canal. I could steal the whole zoo – including the director!"

"But smaller animals are sometimes more valuable!" Isy said. "I think Carrot knows what's happening. He

---

cold-blooded – kaltblütig

claims he tried to tell us. If Amanda could find that recipe, we could maybe work it out."

"Not again!" her friend protested. "It's always my fault! Maybe you picked it up **by accident** and walked off with it."

"What do you mean? I thought you told F.B. that you'd put it in a cook book?"

"Where do you keep your cook books?" Jelly Baby stood up from Isy's favourite armchair and followed Amanda into the kitchen. "My mum's always losing things, too," he reassured her. "We'll find it in no time!"

Isy and Tannhäuser heard rummaging noises in the kitchen, then Amanda squealed with joy.

She reappeared, holding the recipe and looking relieved. "Somehow it had got into my cake-making book by mistake." She held out the newspaper article. "Hagen's amazing. Now he's looking for cigarettes. My dad always hides them."

"It would be more useful if he could help us instead!" muttered Tannhäuser.

They put their heads together, trying to work out the recipe. Isy had never really spoken to Tannhäuser properly before, but he was much nicer than he seemed. He had a really sweet smile. They read the recipe over and over again, even trying to read it backwards. They searched for hidden symbols and held it up against the light. But there was nothing. Just an ordinary recipe – **unless** the reference to pork sausages was a warning about a pig! Was Carrot having a joke **at their expense**?

---

by accident – zufällig;
unless – wenn nicht; at sb 's expense – auf jmds. Kosten

"What's on the other side?" asked Tannhäuser, turning over the cutting. "Maybe the recipe isn't the important bit."

"It's just an Easter nest. Carrot can't have meant that!"

"An Easter nest? It's a bird nest!"

"Well, there are eggs in it," said Amanda, taking the packet of Marlboros from Jelly Baby, who had just walked in, grinning from ear to ear.

"Fantastic! Where were they?"

"Behind the curtain rail. It's an old trick. Nice flat, by the way. How many rooms?"

"Six."

"Six rooms for three people? At our place it's the other way round!"

"There are four eggs in the nest," Tannhäuser interrupted them, trying to focus on the business in hand. "Maybe he's telling us that someone is planning to steal birds' eggs."

"But why?" asked Amanda. "Are they valuable?"

"It depends." Tannhäuser looked **short-sightedly** at the tiny letters next to the black-and-white photo. "It says something about falcons."

"Falcons?" Isy jumped up from Amanda's bed as though she'd been bitten by a tarantula. "Let me see!"

Tannhäuser was right. On the back of the risotto recipe was a nest belonging to a pair of northern falcons. And they'd thought it was an Easter decoration!

Suddenly Isy remembered the TV report about the men waiting to see their sheikh. They'd been holding birds of prey. Surely it couldn't be a coincidence …

"I think I know what this is about!" she said tri-

---

short-sighted – kurzsichtig

umphantly. "Carrot was probably trying to **tip us off**. The zoo's northern falcons are in danger! In the Middle East people will pay at least a quarter of a million dollars for a gyrfalcon. Peregrine falcons are a bit cheaper!" She looked with satisfaction at the surprised faces.

"A quarter of a million?" gasped Amanda. "For a noisy bird!"

"She's right," said Tannhäuser. "I've read about it, too. The criminals are making a big effort, so it would have to be something really valuable. For that amount of money I'd wear a wig, too!"

"Does that mean we're going to have to catch Tengelmann **red-handed** when he's trying to steal a bird?" asked Jelly Baby. "I'd say that's going to be tricky."

"It's enough to have guessed his intention! All we've got to do is prove that he attacked me and Amanda in the zoo." Isy thought for a moment. "We've already taped his voice. And we've got his accomplice's wig. Now we just have to get him to confess. Then we'll have prevented a crime!" She smiled confidently as though she could see herself and Amanda on the front page of the newspaper. The headline would read: "Brave Berlin Girls Prevent Theft at Zoo."

"How are you going to do that?" Tannhäuser sounded doubtful.

"She uses shock tactics," Amanda told him.

Isy nodded. "Do you have a library here, Amanda?"

Her friend shook her head in surprise.

"No problem, we'll just have to use the dining room," decided Isy. "F.B. will be really pleased with us

---

to tip sb off – jmdm. einen Tipp geben;
red-handed – auf frischer Tat

anyway. He won't care about the library. I bet his eyes will fall out of his head when he sees what we're planning to serve him for dinner."

"I don't **get** it," declared Tannhäuser. "Surely you're not planning to invite Tengelmann here?"

"Exactly! And you two" – Isy's finger pointed at Tannhäuser and Jelly Baby – "will ask him to come! You can pretend that you need help with your web project. He knows you, and maybe he'll trust you."

"You're nuts! It'll never work!" Jelly Baby shook his head. "Why do you want to cook dinner for him anyway?"

"It's part of the game."

"When are you planning to do it?"

"The school holidays start next week!

"As for you" – Isy's finger turned to the left and almost **stabbed** Amanda – "you get the chance to cook your dream dinner."

"What kind of dinner?" her friend asked in surprise.

"A dinner for a thief. Just leave the rest to me!"

---

to get sth – hier: mitkommen;
to stab – erstechen

– 19 –

It was obvious that Amanda would have to cook robber-style risotto. What meal could be better **suited to** a thief and a famous criminologist? At least it would be **straight to the point**.

On the day of the big occasion Amanda was standing in the kitchen. Her face was bright red, and sweat was shining on her nose. This wasn't at all how she'd imagined the first day of her holidays. Lying in bed, lazing around and watching soap operas – that was what she'd planned to do. Instead she was **slicing** mushrooms for the main course and telling Isy her doubts. She couldn't believe that it would work.

"It's just another one of your mad ideas! We're going to embarrass ourselves!"

"We'll only embarrass ourselves if you burn the risotto!"

"Don't joke! You know exactly what I'm talking about. What if Tengelmann doesn't show up?"

"He'll be here! Hagen and Reginald will make sure of it!"

"Then what if your shock tactics don't work?"

"They worked before."

"But he's a criminal, Isy! What if he ties us up?"

"I don't think he'll feel like it – not when F.B.'s on the scene."

---

to suit to – passen zu;
straight to the point – direkt, ohne Umschweife;
to slice – in Scheiben schneiden

"OK, what if F.B.'s late then?" Amanda tasted the salad dressing with an unhappy look on her face. "It's making me nervous, Isy. I can't help it!"

"But he promised to be punctual. He can only stay for an hour!" Isy remembered her phone call to F.B., who had accepted the invitation without batting an eyelid. Isy had promised to tell him more about the whispered voice and Carrot's recipe, and had hinted that she had another surprise for him. The criminologist had warned her not to get too excited – he was an Aquarius and couldn't easily be surprised.

"**Chill**, Amanda! You should be pleased that all the trouble at the zoo will soon be over! Where's your **tureen**?"

"Our tureen? We're not having soup, you know!"

"But I need one!"

"It's in the sideboard. But be careful – it's Meißner **china**!"

Isy went into the dining room and fetched a large soup tureen from the sideboard. The table had already been laid. Amanda had used the family's best **cutlery**. It was a pity that the Bornsteins didn't have any silver candlesticks, but then again, they didn't live in an English castle either. There was no doubt that the occasion should really take place in a castle, with a butler, some thick fog and a few **screeching owls**. But the dining room looked impressive all the same.

Amanda's candles would have to twinkle from

---

to chill – sich beruhigen;
tureen – Terrine;
china – Porzellan;
cutlery – Besteck;
to screech – schreien;
owl – Eule

inside the tureen. There was no reason why it should not turn out to be a perfect candlelit dinner. Isy put the china bowl on the table and lifted the heavy **lid**. Then she put her hand into her pocket and placed something inside the tureen that definitely didn't belong there.

She was just trying to move the rubber plant when there was a ring at the door. Tannhäuser and Jelly Baby had arrived.

"He'll be here in half an hour!" they announced proudly.

"We had to tell him that you two are Reginald's cousins," Jelly Baby added with a grin. "We had to explain it somehow."

Tannhäuser's cousins!, thought Isy. Now that was just great …

"But he'll recognize us!" Amanda protested nervously.

"So what? He won't be able to hurt you," said Tannhäuser. "At least not if your Mafia man **knows his stuff!**"

While the boys were still admiring the dining table, Isy arranged the starter on a plate. It had been Amanda's idea to use **ingredients** that were already in the fridge. That way they wouldn't have to waste any money. For their first course she had mixed **tinned tuna**, hard-boiled eggs, black olives, onions and pepper to make a salad Niçoise. She wrapped the freshly baked baguette in a serviette and enthusiastically started to prepare the risotto.

---

lid – Deckel;
to know one's stuff – wissen, wovon man redet;
ingredient – Zutat;
tinned tuna – Thunfisch aus der Dose

"Why did you only set places for four people?" Jelly Baby complained, filling his mouth with a finger-length **garlic** sausage.

"Because there'll only be four of us," Isy said in a friendly tone. "You've been a great help, Jelly Baby!"

"But Tengelmann thinks we'll be here!" Tannhäuser looked disappointed. He prodded Jelly Baby in the ribs. "Come on, big man. You can tell we're not wanted!"

His friend seemed to be frozen to the spot. "Does that mean you're going to eat all this without us?"

"Isy thinks we should handle the matter ourselves." Amanda **stirred** the risotto wildly. The meal was evidently a high-energy affair. "Besides, F.B. hasn't even met you. But we'll save some food for you."

"Don't save anything for me, thanks!" Tannhäuser said coldly. "I don't eat animals."

Amanda's mouth dropped open. Before she could close it, there was a ring at the door. That would be F.B. He must be early. It was the last thing they needed! Isy glanced around in panic. What were they going to do with Tannhäuser and Jelly Baby?

"The **broom** cupboard!" whispered Amanda. The boys made signs of protest as Isy pushed them into the cupboard with the vacuum cleaner and some **scrubbing-brushes**. It wasn't exactly fair, but she didn't want **spectators** – and she certainly didn't want rivals for the prize! She rushed back into the dining room and lit the candles, while Amanda opened the door.

---

garlic – Knoblauch;
to stir – rühren;
broom – Besen;
scrubbing-brush – Schrubber;
spectator – Zuschauer

A minute later Berlin's most celebrated mafia specialist was standing in the dining room. He was wearing a smart tie. "Well, that's what I call a warm welcome!" he said, glancing appreciatively at the table. "Is there cause for celebration?"

"Maybe." Isy politely asked the superintendent to sit down. "We're expecting one more guest, but he might be a little late. We should start without him."

Amanda appeared with the **hors-d'oeuvres**. The criminologist enjoyed his starter and showered Amanda with compliments, but the two girls could hardly swallow a single **chunk** of tuna. They were far too excited.

"What have you done with your parents then?" F. B. asked Amanda. "Have you given them cinema tickets or something?"

"Theatre tickets!" she said in surprise. "It's their wedding anniversary!" Then she raced back to her risotto.

"Is it true that you paid a visit to Patrick Talke?" asked Isy, taking a tiny mouthful of bread. "He was mad at us because of you."

"Yes, Carrot was very helpful indeed!" the superintendent informed her. "Things aren't always as they seem, you know. But he knows more than he's prepared to say."

"He's scared!" said Isy.

The superintendent sighed. "To think that only half an hour ago I was sitting in my office ... And now I'm here, at this wonderful dinner table! What a surprise!"

---

hors-d'oeuvre – Vorspeise;
chunk – Bissen

There's an even bigger surprise to come, thought Isy. Soon he would be showing her criminological instincts a little more respect!

"Amanda!" shouted Isy. "How are you getting on with the risotto?"

"I'll have to add more **stock**. My arm hurts already!" Amanda yelled back.

"The dessert will be delicious, too," Isy promised F.B. "Amanda's an amazing chef. She only started cooking last autumn. Sometimes she dreams that she's on TV, cooking dinner for a famous presenter. Can you guess who it is?"

"I'm not up-to-date with these things, I'm afraid," the criminologist apologized. "By the way, what exactly are we celebrating? Does it have something to do with the surprise that you promised me?"

"Yes," Isy said proudly. "We've solved the case!"

"You mean your *imaginary* case?"

"Just you wait and see!"

"I'm **in suspense**!" F.B. glanced around in satisfaction. "Well, you chose a stylish room. It doesn't always have to be an English castle, does it? Of course, some fog would be nice – and maybe some wind howling through the **chimneys**. Or even some screeching owls. And we'd obviously need a mysterious stranger to knock at the heavy, weathered door!"

At that moment the doorbell rang. The noise was so unexpected that Isy jumped. Even the criminologist looked shocked.

"The risotto's ready!" Amanda announced from the

---

stock – Brühe;
to be in suspense – gespannt sein;
chimney – Kamin

kitchen. "Did you bring a **weapon**?" Isy asked F.B. "I mean, in case we need one."

Then she went into the hallway and asked Mr Tengelmann to come inside. If he recognized her, he hid it well. His smile seemed entirely unsuspecting, and his handshake was self-assured and firm. The man had no idea what was in store for him! Her shock tactics were certain to work.

"Good evening!" she said bravely. Their guest answered in a voice as quiet as a whisper. All of a sudden, she was overcome with panic. She remembered how frightened she'd been when she first played the recording in Mr Knöpfle's office. Her knees were shaking.

She hurried into the dining room and introduced him to the superintendent. "Mr Tengelmann has agreed to help us with our project."

"So you're the fourth guest," F.B. said. His eyes twinkled.

"Bollerbusch! How nice to see you!"

Bollerbusch? Wasn't he called Baltruschat? Isy was confused. But no, he had lots of names to choose from!

Not surprisingly, the latecomer was filled with embarrassment when he saw the dinner table.

"Oh, I'm sorry," he whispered, "I didn't realize ... But your cousin was so determined. He said it was important that I came over. Something about northern falcons, I understand."

"Our cousin had to leave suddenly," said Isy, "but we're working on the project together. Besides, we didn't want to start the main course without you. Isn't that right, Amanda?"

---

weapon – Waffe

Amanda carried in the risotto. Her cheeks were red. Looking nervously at their new guest, she placed the dish of rice on the table. It was topped with pork sausage and smelt delicious.

Tengelmann's small pink scar shone in the candlelight. Amanda shuddered.

"Oh, risotto e salsicciotti!" said Mr Tengelmann admiringly. He was obviously a **connoisseur**.

"Our recipe calls it *robber-style risotto,*" explained Isy. "We got it from your colleague Patrick Talke. The one who was attacked three weeks ago."

"Yes, odd things have been happening at the zoo."

"They're even odder than you think! My friend Amanda and I were attacked, too. We were tied up and locked in an animal pen!"

Mr Tengelmann's eyes **narrowed**. "In broad daylight?"

"Well, I guess it was more like evening," Isy admitted in a small voice. "But still! We seem to be getting in the way of certain people at the zoo. Luckily, we managed to tape a voice. It was pure luck that we recorded it." She peered curiously at the others, but they were concentrating on the robber-style risotto.

"Just heavenly!" Isy **praised** her friend. At that moment she heard a **cough**. It was coming from the broom cupboard. She continued in a loud voice, "Maybe one of you will be able to identify the voice?"

She placed Tannhäuser's tape recorder on the table and Mr Tengelmann's low voice filled the room. "Two

---

connoisseur – Kenner;
to narrow – sich verengen;
to praise – loben;
cough – Husten

girls," he whispered, "a fat one and a skinny one! I'd say they're thirteen or fourteen years old. I noticed them right away because they've been snooping around …" Isy switched off the machine.

"Well, it's certainly an unusual voice!" The famous criminologist flashed a friendly smile at Mr Tengelmann. Finally, thought Isy. At last the penny's dropped. F.B. had better have his gun ready in case Tengelmann made a run for it. She had to take him by surprise.

There was a **tense silence**.

"You stand accused, Mr Tengelmann," she said firmly, "of spying on me and Amanda. What's more, you are under suspicion of attacking your colleague Patrick Talke and of locking me and Amanda in a pen. We're not sure how this is linked to a certain capuchin monkey, but we can reveal the identity of your accomplice. She gave herself away! Amanda, fetch the **spare** head of hair from the rubber plant!"

Amanda's eyes were wide with excitement. She fished the wig from the plant pot and threw it to Isy, who held it under the suspect's nose. "It's time you **came clean**, Mr Tengelmann!"

For a moment there was silence except for the **spluttering** of the candles. Eventually Mr Tengelmann pushed back his plate. "The voice on the tape is mine – I'll happily admit that. But the rest is nonsense. Why on earth would I hit Patrick and lock you up?"

"Because a rich sheikh is waiting for you in the **desert**. I bet he's looking forward to his falcons from Berlin."

---

tense silence – gespannte Stille;
spare – Ersatz-; to come clean – gestehen;
to splutter – hier: knistern;
desert – Wüste

"I'm afraid I'm going to have to disappoint you. There aren't any falcons at the zoo."

"Now you're definitely lying!" Isy sounded confused.

"If you don't believe me, you should check."

Now she was going to have to go all the way. She couldn't allow herself to be silenced. Tengelmann was a hard nut to crack.

"We've been given a tip-off about the theft of some birds!' Isy's fingers trembled as she placed the recipe on the table. "Carrot gave us a clue on the back of this recipe. Falcons' eggs! You may have attacked him, but he was still holding this cutting when we found him. We can't prove anything at the moment, but the police will find you guilty of attacking Carrot, Amanda and myself! You made a serious mistake when your threat was recorded."

She plunged her hand into the tureen and put Amanda's small black tape recorder into F.B.'s hands. He looked at her in astonishment. "We've recorded everything!" She **winked** triumphantly **at** Amanda, who appeared to be frozen to the spot. "I hope you're pleased with us this time, Mr Baltruschat!"

The superintendent raised his eyes to the ceiling.

"My dear Isolde! My dear Amanda! Congratulations on finding my best undercover agent at the zoo! I'm not sure whether to laugh or cry ..."

---

to wink at – zublinzeln

– 20 –

They were back at the little café again, eating pistachio ice-cream. For once they couldn't feel the magic. *Georgio's* mysterious shimmer had gone. Their mood was probably to blame. Signore Georgio lined up a row of grappa bottles on the ebony counter. He could tell that something was wrong.

"Don't you like my ice-cream?" he asked them anxiously. "You've barely eaten anything. You're like a pair of sick cats."

"Your ice-cream is delicious!" Amanda reassured him. "Va bene! That's not the reason why Isy's lost her appetite."

"Molti problemi? Have some pasta! Pasta will make you happy!"

If only it were that simple, thought Isy. This time her embarrassment couldn't be swallowed with a few forkfuls of pasta. Her skin **crawled** every time she thought of how awful her stammered **apology** must have sounded to Mr Tengelmann. Not to mention F.B. The superintendent had been forced to find a new agent for the zoo – it was no use having an undercover agent who wasn't undercover. "Congratulations," Reginald and Hagen had chorused when Isy opened the broom cupboard. "Another fine disaster for the calamity queens!"

It was all her fault. How could she have been so mis-

---

to crawl – hier: kribbeln;
apology – Entschuldigung

taken? Her theory had seemed to make sense! She would never have guessed that Mr Tengelmann's mysterious conversation had been conducted with F.B.! The police agent had found a job at the zoo by pretending to **research** birds and their behaviour. He'd been worried that Isy and Amanda would put themselves in danger by discussing contract crime. That was why he'd wanted to "take care of them", but F.B. had decided to give it more time.

"Everyone makes mistakes, you know," Amanda told Isy. "Anyway, your logic wasn't completely wrong. F.B. was really impressed by the way you handled that granny. Why else would he have congratulated you? He couldn't wait to take the wig away for testing!"

That was true. Up until now the police hadn't had any proof that a woman was involved. F.B. had wanted to know all the details.

"But that's just peanuts!" Isy said. She sounded depressed. "It won't help us to solve the case."

"There's no need for us to solve it!" Amanda **dug** her plastic spoon into Isy's portion of ice-cream and took a spoonful. "Can't we talk about something else? Have you finally spoken to your parents about that language course?"

"There's no point. It's too expensive."

"I thought your mum had a fantastic new job."

"It's not quite as fantastic as she thought."

"Well, at least we've still got Monki!" Amanda gave her a **sly** look. "We could sell him to the travel agency

---

to research – erforschen;
to dig – stechen, graben;
sly – verschwörerisch

for five thousand Euros. That's a fifty per cent **discount**. A real **bargain**! And we'd still be left with a whole heap of cash. What do you think? Shall we call them?"

"Have you got your phonecard with you?"

"Thank goodness!" Amanda **beamed at** her. "I thought you'd never **see sense**!"

As soon as they were in the phone box, she realized her mistake. Isy wasn't phoning the travel agent: she had entered the number for the hospital instead.

"Why are you calling Mr Rimpau of all people?"

"Because we promised to phone him."

"But he's bound to be at home by now."

Amanda was right. The hospital told her that the author had been sent home the day before yesterday.

"Now what?" Amanda put the card back in her pocket.

Good question. It wasn't even lunchtime. They were on holiday, and they had all the time in the world.

"Why don't we visit Mr Tengelmann in the bird house before he has to leave the zoo?"

"Are you completely mad?" cried Amanda. "I'm on holiday! Why would I want to go to the zoo?"

The bird house was **packed** with visitors that morning, but Mr Tengelmann was nowhere to be seen. One of his colleagues, a thin woman with messy hair, told them that he wouldn't be working that week.

"He must be undercover somewhere else," sighed Isy

---

discount – Rabatt;
bargain – Schnäppchen;
to beam at – anstrahlen;
to see sense – zur Vernunft kommen;
packed – voll

in disappointment. It was obvious that she'd intended to **pump him for information**. She kept asking herself why Carrot had given them a tip-off about falcons if there weren't any falcons in the zoo. Maybe it was a secret clue about another valuable species of bird. But how was the mysterious woman involved in the affair? Who was she working with? Had someone else attacked Carrot? Were the same people responsible for locking them up in the goat pen? There were so many questions.

Frustratingly, she wasn't allowed to answer them. The criminologist had told her with **uncharacteristic** strictness that she should leave the detective work to the professionals.

Isy couldn't help checking the benches to see whether an elderly grey-haired woman was knitting in the sun. Of course, their suspect was more likely to be the strawberry-blonde woman who was sitting near the monkey house, wearing a black hat and sunglasses and doing a crossword puzzle. Or she could be the brunette in the trouser suit who was sunning herself near the bird house, and who looked away as soon as Isy stared at her.

"If only we could just talk to them," she said. "I bet I'd recognize her voice straightaway." From the look on Amanda's face she knew it was a bad idea. Her friend seemed determined to follow F.B.'s words of warning. In any case, Amanda was in a hurry to get home. Her mum wanted to go shopping with her. And Isy was supposed to be visiting Granny Dora for their **annual** egg painting ceremony. They always blew the

---

to pump sb for information – hier: ausfragen; uncharacteristic – ungewohnt; annual – jährlich

eggs themselves and painted them, even though you could buy stickers instead.

On their way home they saw Reginald and Hagen in the distance. The boys popped out of the bushes, then disappeared.

"They're ignoring us!" Isy grinned. That was fine by her. They'd helped each other for a while, but now that was over. The boys were their rivals again, just as they always had been. Now it was simply a question of writing the best report on the zoo. Isy was determined to take the prize from under the noses of Jelly Baby and Tannhäuser – and all the others, too.

As they passed the aquarium, they saw Mr Knöpfle climbing the stone steps with a roll of paper under his arm. He vanished inside.

"Quick! Let's go after him! We still haven't apologized," Isy suddenly remembered.

They ran towards the steps. By the time they reached the **foyer**, the zoologist had disappeared through the gates. They waited impatiently with the queue of other visitors until the porter let them in. He stopped them at the last second.

"Hang on! Wait here!" In his hand was a dark blue sports bag that seemed very familiar. "Is this the bag that you've been looking for?"

"That's the one!" Amanda shouted joyfully, **unzipping** it hurriedly. She was beaming as she held up her pink sports kit. "It's all here! Some people are honest after all!"

"Then if you'll just sign here …" the porter said in satisfaction.

---

foyer – Vorraum;
to unzip – Reißverschluss aufmachen

Amanda signed her name and picked up the holdall. The porter handed her an envelope. "It's from the honest person who found your bag," he said cheerfully.

The person in question was Julia Zork. She had written her address and phone number on a cream-coloured piece of card. Her elegant handwriting informed them that she'd spent the past few weeks in Scotland.

"It's her!" cried Amanda. "She was one of the Goths! She probably went on holiday to a Scottish **cemetery**, and now she wants her monkey back! It had nothing to do with the mafia! I told you so, Isy!"

She put the card in her bag and joined Isy in the hunt for Mr Knöpfle. They found him on the **staircase**. He was pinning a poster to the wall.

"What are you doing with that poster?" asked Isy, staring at the photo. "Hey! That's Mr Rimpau!" she exclaimed in astonishment.

"Our press officer is in bed with the flu," said the zoologist, who didn't usually have to pin up posters. "On Easter Sunday we're presenting our Easter treat for grown-up visitors. The author will be reading from his latest crime novel and signing copies of his book. It starts at midday in the aquarium. We couldn't advertise the event any sooner because we weren't sure whether he would be out of hospital in time. Do you know him?"

"He's a friend of ours," Isy said proudly. "Actually, Mr Knöpfle, we're here to say sorry. We really enjoyed our trip to the kitchens. It's such a shame that Amanda suddenly felt sick."

---

cemetery – Friedhof;
staircase – Treppenhaus

"No problem." His blue eyes shone in his tanned face. He looked like a **lifeguard** from a series on TV. Isy was certain that he had strong arms and a mat of blonde hair on his chest.

"Is there an Easter treat for younger visitors, too?" Amanda asked hopefully.

"Easter nests with chocolate eggs! You're welcome to join in the hunt – if you're not too old for that kind of thing."

"Oh, I'd love to, but I'm going to Nuremberg on Easter day." Amanda was sorry to miss the hunt.

"And I'm going to visit my grandma," added Isy. "It's a pity. I would have liked to see Mr Rimpau. Are you a fan of detective novels?"

"Absolutely not!" The zoologist shook his head. "I prefer fairy tales. I collect different stories from around the world. At least in fairy tales the good guys always win."

"I entirely agree with you!" Amanda said softly. "But if Isy had it her way, we'd be chasing criminals all day!"

Mr Knöpfle laughed. "It doesn't surprise me! All that stuff on television is enough to make anyone crazy. At least the zoo is peaceful. You can relax and forget about fictional gangsters and guns!"

Isy smiled to herself. So Mr Knöpfle thought the zoo was peaceful, did he? If only he knew …

---

lifeguard – Rettungsschwimmer

– 21 –

Isy slept fitfully on Saturday night. She tossed and turned in her bed and had all kinds of weird dreams. On Easter Sunday she woke up and couldn't remember a thing. The colourful images had **merged into** a shapeless mess. Whilst Isy was in the shower, the long-awaited Easter-egg hunt **melted** into nothingness. Granny Dora had the flu.

What a terrible start to the day! Now she would have to hunt for her Easter eggs in the living room like Amanda.

"Why don't you *give* us our chocolate instead?" Benedikt asked his parents. "That way you won't have to hide the eggs, and we won't crash into the furniture."

"Don't listen to him!" protested Isy. She didn't want to be given her treats. Easter wouldn't be Easter without an Easter-egg hunt – even if it had to take place inside. Fortunately, her parents agreed with her. The Easter egg hunt took thirty minutes and required all kinds of acrobatic manoeuvres. Then Isy was back at the breakfast table, eating miniature chocolate eggs, with her nose in a book. This year her Easter novel hadn't been hidden under Granny Dora's pear tree.

Isy would have been quite happy to eat chocolate

---

fitful – unruhig (Schlaf);
to merge into – übergehen in;
to melt – schmelzen, hier: sich auflösen

and read all day, but her father left after breakfast to take Granny Dora her egg. Isy decided to leave the house, too. Mr Rimpau would be giving his reading at the zoo. There was no reason why she shouldn't go along. She couldn't wait to see Amanda's expression when she told her. Maybe she'd even find one of Mr Knöpfle's Easter eggs hidden at the zoo.

The chances of Isy finding anything were practically **nil**. The zoo was overflowing with people. The citizens of Berlin were walking through the parkland, while hordes of children raced around looking for Easter eggs. Some of the eggs had been hidden by their parents, some by the zoo and others by well-known supermarkets.

Inside the aquarium Mr Rimpau was reading from his book. His reading glasses were balanced on his nose, and he kept glancing at his audience. Isy decided to wave at him if he saw her. Copies of *One Murder Too Many at the Zoo* had been piled up in towers for him to sign. A bookseller was waiting patiently for the fans to start **queuing**.

The operation had left Mr Rimpau looking thinner. Even his voice didn't sound as firm as usual, thought Isy. But he still knew how to hold the attention of his listeners. Most of them were women. Perhaps one of them had run away from two schoolgirls? Someone in the audience might have taken off her glasses, turned her coat inside-out and thrown her wig in the bin. But which one? That one? Or that one? Or maybe the lady over there …

As she stared at them **intently**, one of the women

---

nil – null;
to queue – Schlange stehen;
intent – durchdringend

turned round. Isy almost **jumped out of her skin**. But it was only one of the keepers from the bird house – the thin one with the messy hair.

There was a short break in which Mr Rimpau drank a glass of water. The keeper came up to Isy with a friendly smile. "Isn't your friend with you today?" she asked.

"You wanted to talk to Mr Tengelmann, didn't you? Well, one of my colleagues mentioned this morning that he's back at the other zoo. A nest arrived in East Berlin yesterday – it's something to do with his research, apparently. In any case, he's left the bird house. We were surprised to hear the news."

"What kind of nest?" Isy asked in excitement.

"It belongs to a pair of rare Peregrine falcons. They've laid four eggs. They're due to **hatch** in a few weeks' time ..."

Isy never heard the end of the sentence. She was running through the building. Her mind was racing, too. So it was true! Carrot's tip-off about the falcon nest was real. The two police agents must have seen that straightaway. Mr Tengelmann had tried to convince her that there weren't any falcons!

Why couldn't he have told her that the nest was at the other zoo? Both zoos were in the same city, weren't they? These days they weren't even divided by a wall. It was obvious that F.B. and Tengelmann had wanted to keep her out of it.

Isy rushed towards the train station. She couldn't help thinking of Amanda. Why did she have to be in Nuremberg right now? Isy needed someone she could

---

to jump out of one's skin – erschrecken;
to hatch – schlüpfen

talk to. Amanda would raise her eyebrows when she told her of her suspicions, but at least she'd listen.

Isy was so wrapped up in the thought of Amanda that she could picture her clearly: she was dressed in a smart Easter outfit, with a short **pleated skirt** and white shirt. Was she hallucinating? Isy closed her eyes in alarm. When she finally dared to open them again, Amanda was still there. She was marching towards the aquarium at high speed.

"Amanda!" Isy yelled in disbelief. "Is that you?" The blonde girl in the red jacket came to a halt and turned round. She still looked like Amanda.

"Isy? But I thought you were at the reading! I phoned your mum and she said ..."

"What are you doing here? Why aren't you in Nuremberg?"

"We didn't get any further than Berlin! Mum drove into the back of another car. It belonged to a priest. She crashed into his **prayer** books!" Amanda tried not to smile.

"Was anyone hurt?"

"Only daddy's most precious possession, the BMW! We drove home **at a snail's pace**. My parents wouldn't stop yelling at each other, so I got out and called you!"

"Perfect timing! Come on, we're off to the other zoo!"

"You're not serious, are you? What's the matter now?"

They ran to the station and got there just as the train to Friedrichsfelde was about to leave. They jumped on

---

pleated skirt – Faltenrock;
prayer – Gebet;
at a snail's pace – im Schneckentempo

and Isy told Amanda the news. "I can't believe no one told us about the falcons in the other zoo!" She sounded outraged.

"They wanted to make sure we didn't get involved."

"Mr Tengelmann might be a double agent! Some undercover agents are gangsters, you know!"

"So what? It's got nothing to do with us." Amanda yawned. "I'm hungry! Are we nearly there?"

East Berlin Zoo was just as busy as the zoological gardens. Parents in smart Sunday clothes were strolling along the paths, while children crawled on their hands and knees through the grass. Thanks to the Easter-egg hunts, most of Easter Sunday was spent staring at the ground. It suddenly **occurred** to Amanda that East Berlin Zoo was quite big. She was prepared to go to the falcons' cage, but no further, she told Isy. But where were the falcons?

Isy didn't know. She had to admit that she hadn't visited East Berlin Zoo for a while. In the end, she decided to ask a keeper. They spotted a grey-haired man who patiently explained that there weren't any Peregrine falcons at the zoo.

"But they've just laid some eggs!" insisted Isy. "Four eggs! Only yesterday ..."

"If that were the case, I think I'd know!"

"Come on," moaned Amanda. "Stop being so stubborn, Isy! There aren't any falcons!"

"But there must be!" Isy said determinedly.

"She's right!" From somewhere behind them came unexpected support.

They turned and stared in astonishment. It was Mr Knöpfle! He was wearing a blue-and-white **bow tie**

---

to occur – in den Sinn kommen; bow tie – Fliege

and carrying a pink cardboard egg. “Isy’s right. There’s a pair of Peregrine falcons here. But no one’s supposed to know!”

“We’re not supposed to know?” Isy was staring at Mr Knöpfle as though his spotted bow tie was about to fly away. “Why not?”

“Falcons are incredibly shy. It would worry them if we were to **put them on display**. They’d never lay eggs. So we hide them from our visitors.”

“Oh!” said Isy. “But why are you here? Business or pleasure?”

“Pleasure!” The zoologist smiled at them.

“That looks amazing!” said Amanda, pointing to the enormous egg wrapped in cellophane. “Who is it for? Your girlfriend?”

“It’s for my sister Marcella.” Mr Knöpfle pulled up his **sleeve** to check the time. “She’ll be waiting for me already.”

“What about the falcons!” cried Isy. “Couldn’t you show them to us quickly? Maybe Mr Tengelmann will be there. He knows us already.”

“They’re kept in an area of the zoo that’s closed to visitors.” Mr Knöpfle looked hesitant. “I may be a zoologist, but that doesn’t give me the right to go wherever I please.” He **swapped glances** with the keeper, who had been listening in silence. The man gave a little nod. “Oh, all right,” said Mr Knöpfle. “I’ll ask if you can visit the falcons. But you’ll only be able to stay for a minute, OK?”

“OK!” Isy beamed at him. “We’re *sooo* grateful!”

---

to put on display – zur Schau stellen;
sleeve – Ärmel;
to swap glances – Blicke austauschen

"In that case, maybe you can help!" Mr Knöpfle dropped the pink egg into Amanda's hands. "Would you give this present to my sister? She's waiting at the exit. Just look for a blonde woman in a red Ferrari. Say hello to her from me and tell her not to bother waiting. I'll be back here in five minutes, all right?" He marched off, while Isy and Amanda hurried on their way.

"Why are you so keen to see the falcons anyway?"

"I don't know. I've got a funny feeling about this."

"I hope we don't have to walk too far because of your funny feeling!" Amanda sounded annoyed with her. She shook the egg **nosily**. "Maybe there are sweets inside!"

"I expect so," said Isy. "What else would you find in an Easter egg?"

"Just think of all those calories." Amanda looked as though she'd like to eat it on the spot.

There was a red Ferrari at the side of the road, just as Mr Knöpfle had described. A slim blonde woman was sitting at the wheel. Isy remembered the photo on Mr Knöpfle's desk. "It's the woman from the picture!" she whispered. "Don't you remember? She's the one who sometimes goes to Philadelphia."

To the woman's astonishment, they knocked on the window, and she opened the door. Amanda placed the giant egg on her lap. "Your brother says 'hi'! You're not to wait for him. He'll catch up with you at home."

"Trust Waldemar!" The woman smiled at them. "Thank you."

She could have said, "We're in for some rain tomorrow" or even "**Beetroots** are good for you". Isy would

---

nosy – neugierig;
beetroot – Rote Bete

have known that voice anywhere. Before her friend knew what was happening, Isy had pushed her to one side and grabbed the egg from the woman.

"Run, Amanda! It's her!"

"What's going on?" asked Amanda in confusion. At that moment the woman grabbed her by the neck and pulled her backwards into the car. She held Amanda tightly. She was very pretty. It was amazing how the wig and the glasses had made her look so old.

"Hand over the egg, Isy."

"Not until you **let go of** my friend!" Isy **hugged** the egg to her body.

"Let's do a deal. Your friend for the egg," said Marcella Knöpfle in a harsh voice; the friendly manner of the old woman had completely disappeared. She'd been acting all along!

Before Isy could decide what to do, she saw Amanda shake her head. It was the only part of her body that the poor girl could move. So Nuremberg still had some heroes! Isy would have liked to hug her.

"Amanda, don't give up! I'm going to fetch some help!" she stammered.

"Leave the police out of it if you want to see your friend again!" Marcella started the engine. "You'll be hearing from me, Isy!" The red Ferrari sped off with Amanda inside.

---

to let go of sb – jmdn. loslassen;
to hug – hier: drücken an

– 22 –

It was just like being in a film. Isy felt as though she was in one of those **gripping** crime movies that showed people getting kidnapped and everyone else knowing exactly what to do. Only in this case Isy didn't have a clue.

She was sitting at her desk, looking at her atlas. The red dot stared back at her, but Philadelphia seemed so irrelevant now. All Isy could think about was Amanda. Perhaps she shouldn't have allowed her to be kidnapped. Maybe she should have done as Marcella had said.

Isy glanced at her bed. The shiny pink egg was **nestled** on her patchwork quilt. She knew it had to be valuable because Marcella had taken Amanda in order to get it back. What could be in an egg that would turn a fairy-tale-loving zoologist into a thief? Mr Knöpfle had always been so nice to them … Isy shook the egg. She even tried sniffing it and holding it to her ear.

Nothing! As far as she could tell, there weren't any animals inside it. It certainly couldn't be hiding a falcon.

She looked anxiously at the time. She'd been home for fifteen minutes, and Marcella Knöpfle hadn't phoned. What would happen if she called the police?

---

gripping – spannend;
to be nestled – hier: liegen

Maybe she should call F.B. or even Amanda's parents ... What would Amanda want her to do?

Isy knew she had to talk to someone, but who could she trust? Mr Rimpau was the obvious choice, but he had only just left hospital. He wasn't strong enough to be hunting down criminals. Perhaps she should ask Reginald and Hagen to help her instead. The boys would have to admit that her theory had been right!

"They've got Amanda!" Isy gasped down the phone. Tannhäuser understood the seriousness of the situation. In no time he and Jelly Baby had appeared at her door.

Isy managed to tell them the story, even though she was in shock. "She told me to leave the police out of it," she **concluded** in a low voice.

The boys nodded in agreement. They'd seen enough crime films to know what that meant. They eyed the egg suspiciously.

"So Marcella said she'd call?" said Tannhäuser. "Does she know your number?"

"Amanda knows it off **by heart**."

"What's this zoologist called again? Mr Knöpfle, isn't it? Why haven't you mentioned him before?" asked Jelly Baby.

"There was nothing to tell! He was always so nice to us. He even showed us the zoo's special kitchens."

"And meanwhile, his sister was snooping around the zoo, disguised as a granny!"

"She was disguised as an *old woman*," Isy corrected him. "There's a difference, you know!"

---

to conclude – beenden;
by heart – auswendig

"I think we should open the egg," said Tannhäuser. "But we need to do it professionally, so no one can tell. I bet there's cocaine inside it!" He turned to Jelly Baby, who nodded in agreement. They carefully got to work.

"What do you mean, cocaine?" asked Isy in alarm. "This is about animals, not drugs!"

"No, you just *think* it's about animals! If there's an animal in there, I'll eat my hat."

Technically, he should have eaten four hats **in one go**! When Reginald Häuser opened the egg, he found four tiny **speckled** eggs. There was no sign of any mysterious bags of white powder.

"Peregrine falcons!" shouted Isy. "I just knew it!"

At that moment the telephone rang. Even Tannhäuser went pale.

Isy's mother called to her from the kitchen, "I expect it's your grandma!" Luckily, Isy got there first.

The voice sounded very cool and **distant**. Isy was told to take the egg to Breitscheid **Square** and get into a green Fiat Uno. "Leave the police out of this," the woman repeated. "I'm sure you're worried about your friend."

"Is Amanda OK?" cried Isy, but Marcella Knöpfle was gone.

Tannhäuser took the phone gently from her hand. "Don't panic! We'll rescue Amanda. We've got to use our heads!"

---

in one go – auf ein Mal;
speckled – gesprenkelt;
distant – distanziert;
square – Platz

Less than fifteen minutes later the boys left the flat. They cycled to the station, and took the train to Breitscheid Square where they looked for a suitable observation post.

Isy set off later, after an argument with her parents. Benedikt had vanished, too, and her parents were left alone for Sunday lunch.

She could understand why they were angry, but she couldn't explain. Her friend's safety was more important than **lamb chops**. Telling her parents about Amanda would put her life in danger.

She made her way to the meeting place, carrying the egg. The boys had closed it so expertly that no one could tell the difference.

Almost everyone smiled at her when they saw the big, pink egg. Isy smiled back. How were they to know that it wasn't an ordinary egg? It was a Trojan horse! A container full of stolen goods ...

She couldn't see the Fiat Uno. It probably wasn't there yet. It didn't matter. There was plenty to look at. Indians from South America often performed on Breitscheid Square. They sang and played drums, warming the cold Berlin air with **fiery** rhythms. Sometimes mime artists painted themselves gold and pretended to be statues. They would stand completely still while the admiring public clapped. Afterwards they would jump down from their platforms and ask the public to pay them for their art.

Isy had seen her first **beggar** there. When the wall came down, her parents had taken her to Breitscheid

---

lamb chop – Lammkeule;
fiery – feurig;
beggar – Bettler

Square. She'd seen a fat woman with two pink poodles and a brightly-coloured bus. It was covered in pictures of lurid green peas and neon carrots. To Isy's eyes it had looked as though the passengers were travelling in an enormous tin of vegetables.

Today the square was as busy as ever. There was a never-ending stream of people heading for the **Memorial Church**. Isy knew that two of the square's visitors had come there specifically to watch over her. But before she could spot Tannhäuser or Jelly Baby, a green Fiat pulled up alongside her. The back door opened. For a moment Isy was tempted to run away. Then she hugged the pink Easter egg to her chest and climbed into the stranger's car. **For Amanda's sake**, she had to be brave!

The car smelt of petrol. It was warm and silent inside. The driver didn't turn to look at her. Isy's view was blocked by the **headrest**, so she couldn't see if the driver was a woman or a man.

Neither of them said anything as they drove through the city. Children were playing, couples were walking and policemen were patrolling the streets. To Isy's astonishment, everyone laughed and waved at them.

As they left Berlin behind them, the driver threw her a black scarf. A low voice ordered her to tie it around her eyes. "If I catch you looking, you'll be **punished**!" the voice hissed sharply. Isy's fingers trembled as she knotted the scarf around her head. Then she pulled it higher over her right eye so there was a tiny gap. She

---

Memorial Church – Gedächtniskirche;
for one's sake – um jmds. willen;
headrest – Kopfstütze;
to punish – bestrafen

peered out at her surroundings. The person turned round, but Isy didn't move a muscle. She sat there quietly.

Now she could see why everyone had waved. She looked with horror through the gap in the scarf. The driver was wearing a rabbit mask!

- 23 -

The trap door was locked and the **skylight** was covered with dust.

Amanda was sitting on the **attic's** only chair. Hands tied together, she stared at the floor. She didn't even look up when the trap door opened and her friend was pushed inside.

Somehow the whole scene reminded Isy of a play. She imagined the **plot**. Amanda was the star of the show, playing a kidnapped young girl. Isy was her best friend, who would break into the attic and use a magic egg to rescue her.

According to the script, she only had to say, "I'm here, Amanda! You're free!", then the two girls would fall into each other's arms, and the audience would applaud. Unfortunately for them, this wasn't a school play. Instead of rushing to **embrace** her, Amanda blinked in exhaustion. "Isy?" she said in surprise.

"I swapped you for the egg," Isy whispered. She proudly showed her friend her **wrists**. Her hands were tied as well. "Does anyone live here?"

"No one," murmured Amanda. "The building's due

---

trap door – Bodentür, Falltür;
skylight – Dachfenster;
attic – Dachboden;
plot – Handlung;
to embrace – umarmen;
wrist – Handgelenk

to be **knocked down**. Marcella told me that I can scream all I like. Only the **pigeons** will hear me!"

"Wow! That woman's a **witch**! But don't worry, we'll soon be out of here!"

"How can you be so sure?"

"Hagen and Reginald followed the car on their bikes. I was brought here in a Fiat Uno. The driver made me tie a scarf around my eyes, but I could still see out. His face was hidden by a rabbit mask, and he talked in a whisper. He wanted me to think he was Mr Tengelmann, but it was a trick! The driver was Waldemar Knöpfle, of course!"

"I couldn't see anything on the way here. Marcella **drugged** me!"

"But you were so brave! Honestly, Amanda, you were amazing!"

"And you behaved like a **jerk**! You should have given her the egg!"

"Hang on, Amanda, you told me not to! You were shaking your head!"

"Only because I couldn't nod! She was holding me really tightly. I bet she's a judo expert or something!"

What? So Amanda wasn't a **heroine** after all! Isy sat down on an old box. She felt confused. Her friend had been shaking her head to tell her that she *wanted* to be rescued. How was Isy supposed to have guessed?

"Why did you have to tell her that you'd recognized

---

to knock down – abreißen;
pigeon – Taube;
witch – Hexe;
to drug – betäuben;
jerk – Trottel;
heroine – Heldin

her?" Amanda hadn't finished complaining yet. "If you hadn't grabbed the egg …"

"Do you realize what's inside it?"

"Chocolate, of course!"

Oh, God. If Isy's hands hadn't been tied together, she would have **clutched her forehead** in despair. "You don't think Marcella would kidnap you for the sake of some chocolate, do you? There's something incredibly valuable inside that egg! That's why we're here."

"Drugs?" guessed Amanda. Her eyes shone with excitement. Even she knew about **drug trafficking**.

"That's what Tannhäuser thought, too. But it's more sophisticated than that. They used the cardboard egg to steal some real eggs! Four tiny little falcon eggs! And guess who helped them to carry the stolen goods out of the zoo … You did!"

"Isolde!" Amanda gasped for breath.

Isy knew what was coming next. She already **regretted** what she'd said. "I'm sorry, Amanda, I …"

"It's too late for that now!" Amanda said crossly. "None of this would have happened if you hadn't insisted on writing about the zoo. If we'd picked Charlottenburg Castle …"

Isy interrupted her. "If we'd picked Charlottenburg Castle, we'd be dealing with an art theft instead!" The fact was, strange things were always happening to them. Surely Amanda knew that?

"But what use are the eggs? I thought they wanted birds!"

---

to clutch one's forehead – sich an die Stirn greifen;
drug trafficking – Drogenhandel;
to regret – bedauern

"They'll wait until the eggs have hatched, of course! Then they'll have four rare Peregrine falcons. Mr Knöpfle knows all about birds, remember!"

Amanda shook her head in disbelief. "It doesn't seem possible that someone who likes fairy tales could be capable of this!"

"You shouldn't believe anything he says! I bet the only thing he studies is the financial exchange rate." Isy snorted. "And he was so good-looking, too."

She got up and walked around the shadowy attic. She was looking for something sharp. She tried to free her hands by rubbing the rope on a rusty metal ladder. Then she saw an old pane of glass in the corner. Perhaps that would work! She would have to be careful though.

"Don't be scared!" she warned her friend and kicked the glass. It cracked and shattered. Thank goodness she was wearing trousers and not a short skirt like Amanda. Nervously she **sawed** through the rope using a sharp piece of glass. She carried it back to Amanda.

"Hold out your hands," she instructed her. Suddenly they heard footsteps from below. Isy raced back to her box and held the glass behind her back. The next moment the trap door flew open and their **would-be** rescuers landed on the floor. They were tied up with rope like a couple of parcels. The door slammed shut, and the footsteps faded. The boys stood up with difficulty. Their feet had been tied as well.

"I thought you were going to rescue us!" said Amanda in shock.

"We nearly did," Tannhäuser told her, "but then this

---

to saw – sägen;
would-be – möchtegern-

idiot here" – he pointed to Jelly Baby – "decided to get himself caught."

"Don't call me an idiot!" thundered Jelly Baby. "Why do you always have to blame me? I'm fed up with your mistakes!"

"Such as?"

"The goat pen, for instance!"

"Keep your mouth shut!" Tannhäuser hissed threateningly.

"The goat pen?" Isy gasped. What was Jelly Baby trying to say? And why did Tannhäuser want to silence him?

"Amanda," she said slowly. She'd had a realization. "Do you remember how F.B. wouldn't believe that we'd been attacked and tied up by the mafia? He said there had to be an alternative explanation. Well, I think we've found it!" She pointed an outraged finger at her classmates.

Jelly Baby tried to defend himself. "It was Tannhäuser's idea! We saw you in the zoo that evening, and he said we should tie you up and put you in a goat pen. We were going to leave you to sweat for half an hour and then rescue you."

"It was **revenge**," explained Tannhäuser. "You told the zoo that we'd been climbing over the fence."

That was a fair point, but it didn't excuse their behaviour.

"So now the truth comes out!" Amanda said triumphantly, then her depression returned. "But we're still locked in."

"We can't use the trap door, of course, but there is another way…" Jelly Baby looked at Amanda's smart clothes. "What's the big occasion?"

---

revenge – Rache

"It's Easter Sunday! I wish my mum could drive properly. Then I'd be in Nuremberg and not in this hole! Where are we anyway?"

"Prenzlauer Berg!" muttered Tannhäuser. "We haven't gone far at all. The man drove round in circles to make sure Isy couldn't guess where she was going. I guess you gave him the egg then?"

"I had to."

"They're bound to be on their way to meet the sheikh already. And we can't even tell the police!" He shook his arms in frustration. "We need a sharp object!"

"Hey presto!" Isy held up the piece of glass. "We'd already thought of that – although I'm not sure you deserve our help!"

"She's right," Amanda said firmly. "**Considering** how mean you were to us in the zoo, we should leave you here."

"You're lucky we still need you," Isy told them. Then she patiently cut through the rope. Amanda rushed to her rucksack as soon as she was free. She pulled out a lunchbox.

"Emergency rations!" she said, putting a bread roll into her mouth. "Does anyone want some?"

Tannhäuser nodded, so she threw him an egg. It had been dyed red.

"Here! Don't tell me you don't eat eggs either!"

"I don't eat *chickens*. I never eat meat."

"Is it something to do with Richard Wagner?"

"Wrong! It's Paul McCartney who doesn't eat meat!"

Jelly Baby snorted. "You're just scared of getting

---

considering – wenn man bedenkt

mad cow disease! Why don't you admit it?" With Isy's help, he tried to push open the skylight. His face went redder and redder, and at last the window gave way. "Anyway, what if all those vegetables give you mad potato disease instead?" He looked at the skylight in satisfaction. "OK, let's go! Come on, roly-poly, I hope you'll fit!"

Before Amanda realized what was happening, Isy was pushing her through the skylight. Screaming and kicking, she arrived on the roof where she and her rucksack were pulled to safety by Jelly Baby's strong arms.

"Are you all completely mad?" screamed Amanda. "I've got **vertigo**!"

"In that case," Jelly Baby advised her, "I recommend you don't look down."

Isy tried to reassure her. "We've got no choice, Amanda. Either we escape over the roof, or we spend the holidays in an attic. You don't want to be stuck here forever, do you?"

Tannhäuser was the last to climb out. All four of them were standing on the roof. A **damp** breeze was blowing around their heads. There was a cloudy sky above them and an empty courtyard below. A **tabby** cat crept lazily over the **cobbles**.

Getting down from the roof was going to be more difficult than Jelly Baby had thought. There was no sign of a fire escape. The neighbouring roof was lower

---

mad cow disease – Rinderwahnsinn;
vertigo – Höhenangst;
damp – feucht;
tabby – getigert;
cobble – Pflasterstein

than this one. They were going to have to climb down there instead.

With hesitant steps, they crossed the short distance to the edge. Tannhäuser was the first to jump. He helped Isy on to the flat roof, and the two of them pulled a white-faced Amanda across the gap. Jelly Baby followed behind her, carrying her rucksack.

"We'll have to climb onto the window **ledge**," he said. "From there we'll be able to get to the balcony."

Considering his weight, it was **astonishing** how confidently he moved at that height. Tannhäuser, by contrast, had to force himself not to be scared. Isy could feel her heart beating wildly. That was OK though. She couldn't wait to describe her crazy adventures to the rest of the class. 7b would listen in respectful silence. No one would have done anything near as exciting as spending Easter on a roof! Even Trischi would have to congratulate them.

"I can't walk along a window ledge!" announced Amanda, holding on to the chimney. "Call the fire brigade instead!"

"We can call all we like – but I don't suppose they'd hear!"

Jelly Baby helped Amanda to take a few steps forwards. His touch was surprisingly gentle. "Can you see that balcony down there? That's where we're heading. Just don't look down! Follow me and walk slowly along the ledge. This isn't the North face of the Eiger, you know!"

"I've got nothing to hold on to!"

---

ledge – Sims;
astonishing – erstaunlich

"Hold on to the **gutter** – but be careful not to pull it off!"

"I'll never make it," murmured Amanda. Isy could picture her during gym lessons at school – she always **flapped** like a nervous chicken.

"It's only another five or six metres, and then you'll be safe!"

"I'm not going to make it! I'm bound to fall!" Soon Amanda was creeping nervously along the narrow ledge. Isy bit her nails as she watched her friend follow Jelly Baby. She moved in **slow motion**, walking behind him like a pale shadow.

They reached the balcony and he pulled her over the railings. Then Isy stepped onto the ledge. Amanda must have been terribly scared! They were three floors above the ground. Thank goodness her parents couldn't see her! She stepped onto the balcony and gave a sigh of relief. Her legs felt like jelly. She helped Tannhäuser to safety, then she **pinched** her friend's pale cheeks. "You were amazing, Amanda!"

Jelly Baby was already working on the next step. He pushed his front door key between the balcony doors. The two wooden doors sprang open, and Jelly Baby walked into the flat. "Happy Easter!" he shouted. "Do you mind if we use your phone?"

---

gutter – Dachrinne;
to flap – flattern;
slow motion – Zeitlupe;
to pinch – kneifen

– 24 –

There was no reply. The flat was empty. Its **occupants** were probably spending Easter with family or friends. Or maybe they'd gone on holiday or taken the dog for a walk.

Soon they were confronted with the next problem. The flat had no phone.

"Everyone uses mobiles these days," Tannhäuser said knowledgeably.

They were standing in the hallway, trying to work out what to do. Isy looked at the sideboard. It had been decorated with fresh **birch** twigs and brightly coloured eggs. They were the prettiest eggs that Isy had ever seen. But surely **circumstances** wouldn't force her to spend Easter Sunday admiring other people's eggs?

"We'll have to call for help!" Tannhäuser muttered softly.

He described the plan: they would stand at the kitchen window and call attention to themselves by shouting, "Help! This is an emergency. Call the police!" or "Hello, down there! We can't get out. Fetch a **locksmith**!" The idea didn't work. Most people were at home, eating Easter cake. In any case, no

---

occupant – Bewohner;
birch – Birke;
circumstances – Umstände;
locksmith – Schlosser, hier: Schlüsseldienst

one took them seriously. They either waved back and laughed, or told the four classmates to stop messing around.

"You youngsters should be ashamed of yourselves," shouted one elderly gentleman as he walked down the street with his grandchildren. "It's Easter Sunday and you're still causing trouble. I've a good mind to call the police!"

"Oh, please do!" Amanda begged him. It was no good. The man disappeared angrily into his house.

"It's hopeless," Isy decided. She sat down unhappily on the cushions of a Biedermeier sofa. They were trapped again. In the attic their exit had been blocked by two metal bars, but now a high-tech lock separated them from freedom.

In the meantime Marcella and Waldemar Knöpfle would be sitting in the departure lounge of a Berlin airport, waiting to fly into the desert with an enormous pink egg. And no one could stop them!

They had no means of **alerting** the police, but surely there was something they could do? Isy had no intention of spending the night in a flat that didn't belong to them! Besides, there was a peculiar smell of dried fruits and leaves. Where was Amanda?

Isy heard the toilet flush. A canary was chirping cheerfully in the kitchen. Tannhäuser stuck his head around the door. "Guess what? There's a fax machine in the study!"

"Do you think we could fax the police?"

"No idea!"

"I know! Mr Bornstein's got a fax machine!" Isy ran out of the living room to bang on the bathroom door.

---

to alert – alarmieren

"Do you know your dad's fax number?" she called out to Amanda.

"Sure, but the machine won't be on. We're supposed to be in Nuremberg." Amanda had just weighed herself and was delighted to see that she was one kilogram lighter than usual. "We could always fax Ruky though."

Ruky? Did Amanda know his number? That was odd ... She must have been in touch with him since they'd left Altgrünheide. Well, she certainly hadn't mentioned it! Isy watched sadly as Amanda wrote down the number. Her best friend was keeping secrets from her!

"What do you think we should say?" Amanda asked Tannhäuser.

"Just tell him you can't wait to see him!" said Isy.

"What's that supposed to mean?"

"Or tell him to steal a Fiat and get us out of here! He's a professional, isn't he?"

"He doesn't steal Fiats any more!" Amanda said proudly.

"Has he moved on to BMWs instead?"

"There's no need to be nasty, Isy. Just tell us the address of this place!"

"I'm not **psychic**, Amanda."

"Well, he can't come to fetch us if he doesn't know where we are!"

Isy gave her a cross look, then jumped up and ran back to the living room. She should have realized that they needed the address. Maybe there would be some mail on the window ledge or something. She sorted through a pile of newspapers and flyers until she finally

---

to be psychic – hier: telepathische Kräfte haben

found an envelope with the occupant's name and address. Now they were ready at last.

"36 Blumenstraße, Prenzlauer Berg. The Krauses live here. **Remind** him to bring a **skeleton** when he comes!"

"A skeleton?" said Amanda in confusion.

"A **skeleton key**, you idiot! How else is he supposed to get in?" Isy glared at Amanda as though she were a beetle. "Why are you always so slow? It's maddening!"

"Whoa!" Amanda breathed out in surprise. "What's your problem, Isy? Are you mad at me for phoning Ruky?"

"You could have told me about it! I would have told you. But I'm just stupid, I guess."

"It wasn't important, Isy. It was nothing. Just a chat."

"In that case, there's no reason for not telling me!"

"OK, sorry, I forgot!"

Amanda pouted and turned her back to Isy. She fed the piece of paper into the machine and waited for the precious "OK" message to appear. With any luck, Ruky would be home and could get hold of a car.

Jelly Baby and Tannhäuser looked bored. They were flicking through the channels on TV. Amanda had started reading the latest celebrity **gossip**, so Isy sat down on the sofa alone. She was determined to make Amanda **suffer** – she'd be sorry that she'd ever kept secrets!

She checked the bookcase and found a book about

---

to remind sb – jmdn. erinnern;
skeleton – Skelett;
skeleton key – Dietrich;
gossip – Klatsch;
to suffer – leiden

spying. Soon she was reading in astonishment about umbrellas that could turn into guns, belts that contained hidden cameras, and biscuit tins that used Morse code. She found it difficult to concentrate though. Amanda couldn't focus either.

"Do you think they've arrived in the desert?" she asked.

Technically, Isy wasn't talking to Amanda, but she couldn't help answering anyway. "They won't have got there yet. We're bound to have **delayed** them. They weren't expecting us to get involved."

"By now those two **crooks** will be escaping. I can't believe we're just **twiddling our thumbs**!" Jelly Baby groaned in frustration. "Maybe I should shout 'Fire!' from the balcony. I bet someone would pay attention to that!"

"Don't be an idiot!" said Tannhäuser. "You could be arrested for disturbing the peace. It's a **criminal offence**."

It was too late. Jelly Baby had disappeared outside. To Isy's surprise he was back within seconds.

"What does Knöpfle look like underneath that mask?" he asked nervously. "He's not blonde, is he?"

"Blonde?" Isy nodded. "Why?"

"I think he's in the attic. He's peering out of the skylight!"

"What?!" Isy sounded incredulous. She tried to push her way past Jelly Baby. "I'll believe it when I see it!"

---

spying – Spionage;
to delay – aufhalten;
crook – Gauner;
to twiddle one's thumbs – Däumchen drehen;
criminal offence – Straftat

Jelly Baby blocked her path. "What if he sees you? I don't suppose he's here to look at the view!"

Oh, hell! What was Knöpfle doing here? Isy stepped back into the living room in confusion. Amanda groaned unhappily and grabbed hold of her bag. "Why isn't he in the plane?" she cried. "I thought he was supposed to be taking those eggs to the sheikh. He should have left by now!"

"Perhaps he lets his sister take charge of the deal," Isy murmured. Amanda pulled a carefully wrapped salami out of her bag. Nothing and no one could ruin that girl's appetite!

Amanda was right though. What was Knöpfle up to? Was he planning to set them free? That would be risky for him, now they knew he'd committed a crime. Maybe he was feeling guilty ...

"Talking of aeroplanes," said Tannhäuser, who was inspecting the Krauses' CD collection. He held up a silvery disk. "The overture to the *Flying Dutchman*! Fantastic! I think I'll put it on."

"Are you c-c-completely mad?" stuttered Amanda. "We're in fear of our lives and all you care about is opera music!"

"I'd rather listen to opera than melodrama, thank you very much! What are you worried about? No one's going to find us here!"

At that moment Isy spotted a shadowy figure on the balcony. The doors opened before she could warn them.

Everything seemed to happen in slow motion.

Isy saw Jelly Baby reach for the remote control. He stopped mid-movement, paralysed with fear. Meanwhile, Tannhäuser had dropped the *Flying Dutchman* and was hiding behind the sofa. A bowl crashed to the floor, and Isy realized that she had instinctively ducked behind the bookcase. A powerful aroma of dried leaves and fruit rose from the carpet where the autumnal potpourri was **strewn**.

Only Amanda had **stood her ground**. She was positioned behind the **intruder**, out of sight. Suddenly she let out an incomprehensible war cry and swung her salami with all her might. The man crashed to the ground like a fallen tree.

"Fantastic!" shouted Isy. "Amanda, you're a star!"

In no time the two boys were back in action.

"Now that's what I call **classy**!" said Jelly Baby admiringly. He reached out to touch the salami, but pulled his hand back just in time. The partially-wrapped, **biodegradable** weapon was a cactus, not a sausage! It had already been used as a weapon once before.

"I never go anywhere without Aeschylus!" its owner exclaimed. "Luckily, I remembered that I'd put it in my rucksack!" She prodded the man with her shoe. "He'll need a good **pair of tweezers**!"

Working together, they expertly rolled him on to his side. A second later they had to rush to catch Amanda. She was suddenly feeling faint. How was she to know that she'd knocked out Berlin's leading mafia specialist? The pale-faced man on the carpet was Fred Baltruschat himself. Isy looked at the lifeless body in disbelief. What on earth was he doing there?

"It's F.B.!" she explained to the boys. "The criminologist. Quick, get some water!"

---

to be strewn – verstreut sein;
to stand one's ground – seinen Mann stehen;
intruder – Eindringling;
classy – klasse;
biodegradable – biologisch abbaubar;
pair of tweezers – Pinzette

"You said it was Knöpfle," stammered Jelly Baby. Tannhäuser fetched the kettle from the kitchen. His face looked grey.

"You only asked if he was blonde!" Isy protested. "I can't help it if everyone's blonde!" She poured cold water over F.B.'s pale forehead.

They heard a noise at the front door. That was all they needed. The Krause family was coming home!

"What's going on?" asked Fred Baltruschat, sitting up with a jolt. He was back on the job straightaway. His blue eyes tried to make sense of the situation. "I suppose you knocked me out then?" He grinned. "That was some **crack** on the head you gave me!"

He put up his hand to feel his head, but quickly withdrew it, groaning with pain.

"Those are the **prickles** from Amanda's cactus," said Isy in embarrassment. "We're really sorry. We thought you were someone else! It all happened so quickly."

"Didn't you do the same thing to my old friend Rimpau?" growled the detective. "I seem to remember him telling me." He pulled his mobile out of his pocket. "I'll have to ring the station and tell them that you're safe. They need to focus their efforts on Knöpfle!"

"So you know about Knöpfle?" Isy said in surprise. "Tell your colleagues that Knöpfle and his sister are at the airport or maybe even in the air. The **booty's** hidden in a big, pink Easter egg!"

"His sister? Do you mean to say that ...?" The famous criminologist was speechless. He lowered his mobile.

---

crack – Schlag;
prickle – Stachel;
booty – Beute

"That's right! Knöpfle's working with his sister Marcella – the 'old' woman at the zoo. Isy recognized her just before she kidnapped me!" explained Amanda, who'd only just opened her eyes.

"Wow!" said the superintendent. "Do you have any more surprises for me?"

"Sure! Say hello to Ruky König!" A young man with dark eyes and dark braids had joined them. Thanks to his skeleton key, he seemed to have appeared out of nowhere.

"We told you about him before, remember? He's the one who grows vegetables to the sound of Haydn. He's a friend of Mr Rimpau's, too!"

"What kind of music is he playing today?" asked F.B. whilst tapping a number into his mobile.

"I'm just in charge of the taxi!" Ruky König flashed him a smile. "It's only an A-class Mercedes, but I didn't have time to break into any really flashy cars. It's pretty fast though!"

F.B. groaned. "My mind must be playing tricks on me. I guess that's what comes of colliding with a cactus!" He took a few steps towards Ruky. "I haven't seen you, Ruky. I don't remember you ever being here at all. Now beat it! But leave the Mercedes behind. It's staying here!"

"What's his problem?" asked Ruky. He stepped backwards in confusion. "Doesn't the old granddad want to come, too?"

"That's Superintendent Baltruschat!" Isy gave a sigh. "I've no idea how he found us!"

"What! He's a policeman?" Ruky ran down the hallway. "You two are a liability! Next time fax someone else for help!"

"He's a nice guy really!" Amanda shouted after him. "Completely human. Please don't go!"

It was too late. The front door slammed shut.

"Ruky's got a good heart." Isy sighed again. "He was only trying to help. We'd really **appreciate** it if he doesn't get into any trouble for this." She fell silent and listened to the instructions that F.B. was giving on the phone.

"According to the kids, the eggs are hidden in a big, pink Easter egg." F.B. paused for a moment and turned round. "That's right, isn't it?"

Isy exchanged knowing looks with Tannhäuser and Jelly Baby.

"Oh, yes," she said **mischievously**. "But let's hope that the sheikh likes chocolate eggs, too!"

---

to appreciate sth – etwas schätzen;
mischievous – verschmitzt

– 25 –

It was an evening of the kind that Signore Georgio liked best. All the tables in his café were full, and in all four corners people were eating, drinking and chatting.

He always saved the table between the window and the counter for his favourite customers. Right now it was occupied by his young friend Amanda and her pretty companion with the dark curls. The third chair was taken by a policeman whom Signore Georgio had never seen before. The three of them were so busy talking that they hadn't even ordered!

Signore Georgio wondered whether they were discussing the newspaper article that was lying on their table. The photo showed Signoritas Amanda and Isolde with two boys from their class. The café owner had read the article that morning while he was drinking his espresso. The four schoolkids had succeeded in putting a stop to the criminal **antics** of the Knöpfle duo who had been **plaguing** German zoos for some time.

According to the article, the kids had even managed to rescue some precious falcon eggs. Isy had hidden the real eggs in her bed and had tricked the Knöpfles into taking some chocolate eggs instead. Thanks to their help, the bird smugglers had been arrested before they could leave Tegel airport on their way to Oman. Eccellente! What fabulous customers he had!

---

antic – Posse;
to plague – plagen

"Had you been watching Knöpfle for long then?" asked Isy. F.B. informed her that he'd received an anonymous tip-off, but they'd been unable to find any proof.

"It was only thanks to your help that we found out he was working with his sister Marcella."

"I see, so you decided to get Mr Tengelmann to keep an eye on him." Isy grinned. "Although I don't suppose he's called Mr Tengelmann at all."

"Of course, he isn't!"

"What does Carrot have to do with all this?" Amanda asked impatiently.

"Patrick Talke used to work at Rostock Zoo. He was there for two years, then one day a pair of gyrfalcons disappeared without a trace. Waldemar Knöpfle was working there, too – he was in charge of building an aviary like the one in Berlin. Carrot couldn't help noticing that Knöpfle was driving a pretty expensive car – a Ferrari. Some of Knöpfle's other colleagues had commented on his **frequent** visits to casinos and expensive bars. But everyone knew that he had **wealthy** parents in Stuttgart."

"Isn't it time that we ordered?" suggested Amanda, conscious of her empty stomach. They hadn't had anything to eat since breakfast. That morning they had collected Monki from the travel agency and returned him to the grateful Goth. "I'll have Saltimbocca – **veal** with ham and egg. And for dessert ..."

"Don't you want to know who was responsible for attacking Carrot?" asked Isy.

---

frequent – häufig;
wealthy – wohlhabend;
veal – Kalbfleisch

"Sure, but that doesn't mean I have to starve!"

The superintendent was used to their **squabbling**. He chuckled. "Carrot's suspicions were raised when he found out that Knöpfle had worked as an assistant at Leipzig Zoo. It was just after the wall came down, and a number of precious birds had disappeared.

When your friend bumped into Knöpfle again, this time at Berlin Zoo, he decided to keep an eye on him. That was about a year ago. He couldn't find any proof though. In the end, he decided that playing detective was too much like hard work. He gave up – but not without leaving an anonymous tip-off with the police."

"What about the attack in the nocturnal house?" probed Isy. "If Mr Knöpfle wasn't guilty of hitting him, it must have been Marcella!" She told F.B. how she had watched Carrot make his way cautiously through the crocodile house. It had been obvious that he was scared of being followed.

"Of course, he was being followed! But he wasn't being trailed by gangsters." F.B. gave a knowing smile.

Apparently, Carrot had been right to be nervous. He was in a relationship with a colleague's girlfriend and was secretly planning to go on holiday with her to the Maldives. The attack had been carried out by the jealous colleague. Carrot had **grasped** the situation right away and had decided to disappear – but this time without his colleague's girlfriend, and not to the Maldives.

"Unbelievable!" gasped Amanda. "Can we order now?"

---

squabbling – hier: Geplänkel;
to grasp – begreifen, erkennen

"Not until someone tells me how Knöpfle stole the eggs!" protested Isy.

"I thought I was being taken out for a meal, not a conference!" Amanda gave a loud groan. Even so, she listened carefully to what the superintendent had to say.

In his opinion, it would have been easy for the zoologist to **gain access** to the eggs. After all, he was a trusted member of staff and no stranger to the zoo. There would have been nothing unusual about him taking a professional interest in the nest.

"No one apart from Tengelmann suspected what he was up to." The superintendent explained how Mr Tengelmann had **volunteered** to look after the falcons over the Easter holidays, in the knowledge that Knöpfle would have to act while the eggs were still fresh. Older eggs were more difficult to transport and had to be kept in special containers to **ensure** they stayed warm.

"Knöpfle knew that Mr Tengelmann was watching him, didn't he?" Isy burst out. "Whilst he was driving me to the attic, he kept talking in a whisper. He wanted me to think it was Tengelmann under the mask!"

"Isy, I'm impressed! Yes, Marcella Knöpfle had been watching the zoo closely and had found out that Tengelmann was working undercover. Neither he nor anyone else paid any attention to her because of her disguise. We only realized that Knöpfle had a female accomplice when you told us about the wig." The superintendent sipped his red wine.

---

to gain access – Zugang bekommen;
to volunteer – sich freiwillig melden;
to ensure – sicherstellen

"In any case, Knöpfle had been warned by his sister about Tengelmann. He knew that Tengelmann always drank a thermos flask of tea for breakfast. That was all the information he needed. He only had to add a few knock-out drops to the flask. The rest was child's play. Fritz Tengelmann drank his tea as usual, and collapsed. Waldemar Knöpfle instantly swapped the four real eggs for four fake eggs of a similar size and colour. He hid the real eggs in an Easter egg. You won't find a better hiding place than that at Easter!"

"What happened when Mr Tengelmann woke up? Did he realize what had happened?" Amanda was so excited that she'd forgotten to mention food.

"Tengelmann's a professional agent, remember! But Knöpfle had vanished without trace."

"Maybe Mr Rimpau will write a new novel when he hears our news!" Isy said excitedly.

"Why don't you ask him?" F.B. suggested. To Isy's great surprise, the crime writer sat down at their table.

"Good work!" the latecomer praised them, pointing to the photo. "What clever friends I have!"

We didn't keep our promise, thought Isy. He's bound to be cross.

But Mr Rimpau was more interested in hearing about what had happened to Monki.

"We've taken him back. His owner had picked up the wrong bag. It happened whilst we were standing next to the shark tank. She was really pleased to see him!"

Isy couldn't help grinning. Amanda had looked so disappointed when she'd found out that Julia Zork didn't sleep in a coffin. The pretty Goth had a perfectly ordinary bed and didn't even own any crucifixes or black candles.

"How did you know where to find us?" Isy asked F.B.

"On Easter Sunday someone rang up to complain about four noisy young people in Prenzlauer Berg. From the description, the two girls sounded oddly familiar."

"So you decided to take a look for yourself!"

"Thank goodness you did!" Amanda looked casually at F.B.'s black shirt. "Is that Armani, superintendent?"

"Mail order!"

"Well, it's very chic," Amanda said **graciously**. "You should wear black more often."

"Shush," Isy hissed at her. "Why don't you ask Mr Baltruschat or Bauernöppel or Bollerbusch or whatever his name is why he decided to crawl over the roof?"

"Intuition!" the superintendent said.

When he had arrived at the **scene of the incident**, he had immediately noticed the empty house. His instinct had told him to take a closer look. The front door of the house had been **bolted**, but the skylight was open. The cut ropes and the splinters of glass had told him the rest of the story, and he only had to follow it to its conclusion.

"That's how I ended up on the roof, wondering where you could have got to!"

He gave a detailed description of how he had walked to the edge, jumped on to the balcony and been greeted by an aggressive cactus.

"Where did you get your war cry from?" asked Isy.

"I came up with it on the spot," admitted Amanda.

---

gracious – gnädig;
scene of the incident – Ort des Geschehens;
to bolt – verriegeln

"Can we order now? Signore Georgio keeps looking at us."

"We haven't told the superintendent about the goat pen. You'll never guess who locked us in!" said Isy.

"Are these the culprits?" he asked, pointing to two boys who had just walked in.

"You didn't invite *them*, did you?" mumbled Amanda.

"Of course, I did! They helped to save the falcons, too!"

The superintendent signalled to Signore Georgio that they were ready to order. Then Tannhäuser and Jelly Baby joined them at the table and proudly described how the newspaper article had changed their public image.

"For once it's something positive about me!" Jelly Baby said in satisfaction.

Amanda had to admit that her parents had been horrified. They still weren't happy about her returning to the zoo.

"But we won't win the trip to Philadelphia if you can't go to the zoo!"

"We're going to win anyway!" chorused Tannhäuser and Jelly Baby.

"In your dreams!" said the girls in a kind of duet.

"We could beat you with our eyes closed!"

"We could beat you with our eyes closed *and* our hands tied!"

Mr Rimpau interrupted them. "What's the matter?" he asked. "I thought you made a great team. Why don't you join forces for the project?"

"We haven't really decided what to write," Isy said. She was avoiding the question.

"Neither have we." Tannhäuser avoided it, too.

"I've got an idea!" Mr Rimpau beamed at them.

"Write a detective story about the zoo. You've got plenty of experience!"

A detective story? That would be cool! But working together with two boys who had locked them in a goat pen … Isy could tell that Amanda was thinking the same. Jelly Baby and Tannhäuser exchanged a meaningful look.

"I've got more good news!" announced the superintendent.

More good news? Isy was already feeling pleased. That morning her mother had told her that she'd found a last-minute place on a computer course.

"My colleagues at the police would like to give you a reward in recognition of your exemplary civil courage. You can spend the money on your trip across the **pond**. Now all you have to do is work together and win!"

"Go on, it won't be that bad!" Mr Rimpau **urged** them.

At that very moment Isy and Amanda were overcome with a coughing fit, while Tannhäuser and Jelly Baby were busy sneezing violently. They didn't stop until a plate of bruschetta landed on their table. It smelt delicious.

"A present from the management!" Signore Georgio grinned at them. "Buon appetito!"

During the summer holidays four postcards with a view of the Brandenburg countryside were posted through four different letterboxes. Mr Rimpau, Fred Baltruschat, Patrick Talke and Ruky König all received the same message:

---

pond – Teich;
to urge – drängen

"Greetings from Philadelphia! We made it! Our detective story beat all the other reports to win first prize! It's amazing here. There's so much to see, and the computer centre has taught us loads. Unfortunately, we're not speaking as much English as we'd hoped since our Philadelphia is only forty kilometres to the east of Berlin. Trischi had known all along – he was probably laughing at us all the time. Boston's pretty close, too, or so we hear. Tomorrow we're going for a bike ride with the boys. Love,

Isy and Amanda